Walking i

Franz Hessel was born in 1
and grew up in Berlin. Af
in Paris, moving in art
translated Proust with
by Casanova, Stendh
the fashion journal
Henri-Pierre Roc
film *Jules et Jim.*
diplomat and
Vous! (Time
shortly afte

Amand
of Re
base

WALKING
IN BERLIN

FRANZ HESSEL

Translated by Amanda DeMarco

SCRIBE
Melbourne • London

Scribe Publications
18–20 Edward St, Brunswick, Victoria 3056, Australia
2 John St, Clerkenwell, London, WC1N 2ES, United Kingdom

First published in English by Scribe 2016
Translation © Amanda de Marco 2016
First published in German under the title *Spazieren in Berlin* in 1929

Typeset in Dante MT Std by the publishers
Printed and bound in the UK by CPI Group (UK) Ltd, Croydon CR0 4YY

Scribe Publications is committed to the sustainable use of natural resources
and the use of paper products made responsibly from those resources.

9781925321128 (Australian hardback)
9781925228359 (UK hardback)
9781925307337 (e-book)

CiP records for this title are available from the British Library
and the National Library of Australia.

scribepublications.com.au
scribepublications.co.uk

Contents

Foreword
by Amanda DeMarco

'To this day, there is no better Berlin travel guide,' proclaimed an article in the *Tagesspiegel* more than 80 years after the original publication of *Walking in Berlin*.[1] What is it about this book that captured the spirit of the city in such a lasting manner?

Or perhaps to put it more accurately: a recurring manner. A critical success upon its publication in 1929, *Walking in Berlin* was largely forgotten after the Second World War. It was rediscovered in Germany in the 1980s after it was revealed that the love triangle in the book and film *Jules et Jim* was based on a relationship that Hessel and his wife Helen Grund had had with the novelist Henri-Pierre Roché (a fact that had been withheld from the public until Grund's death). Another wave of attention came in 2011, when Hessel's work entered the public domain. The Weimar-era flowering of culture and relaxed social mores depicted in the book certainly resonate with our contemporary conception of the city. Hessel's Berlin rings true to us today.

He also chose a format that is particularly natural to modern urban experience. The essays are divided geographically, each covering a portion of the city — that is, they are more or less a series of walks (or, occasionally, drives). Abounding in detail, they are very nearly as stimulating as the real places they

---

1   Peter von Becker. 'Der Flaneur als Auge der Stadt'. *Tagesspiegel*, 23 May 2011.

describe, and the most fruitful way to explore them might be the way you would explore a city, taking a foray through one neighbourhood today, another tomorrow.

Hessel's knowledge of city history was extensive, gleaned from an art-history education and an avid personal interest in the cultural sediment that had accumulated around him. It is evident in these pages that history was alive and present for him, visible in the architecture. All it took was a glimpse of a statue or bridge or gate to send Hessel conjuring up the figures and era that produced it.

Berlin was rapidly modernising in the 1920s, and Hessel's enthusiastic depiction of this new Berlin forms the counterweight to his historical reveries. Whether speeding down Kurfürstendamm (with a lady driver!), taking a tour of a new factory, or watching a group of young women prepare for a night on the town, the breathless pace of his descriptions reveals the new heartbeat of a populace that was cathartically shaking off the trauma of the First World War, while frantically grasping for economic stability.

For all of the historical and social background that *Walking in Berlin* provides, its pages are remarkably free of political commentary. Hessel's ideal was to observe and record. He wanted to detail the city as if he were seeing it for the first time, to truly skim its surface. This might involve some social analysis, but always as a natural outgrowth of what he is observing at any given moment, rarely as a pre-formed opinion. When he does note his own response to his surroundings, it is often wonder.

This is perhaps the most evident expression of Hessel's

personality in the book. Contemporaries described him as gentle, kind-spirited, reticent, at times feminine—all characteristics he himself echoed and seemed to take on as a sort of unworldly poet-persona. The role of the observer simply suited him. However, we must regard it as an irony that he chose not to be more socially critical in his writings; Jewish by birth (though he converted), the last decade of his life was darkened by the growing shadow of National Socialism, and he died in exile in France in 1941, greatly weakened after his release from an internment camp.

It is clear (from this book, as well as his other writings) that in the era these essays were written, Hessel did not believe the Nazis would wreak the havoc that they eventually did (and did not accept this until rather late, ignoring his friends' urgings to flee until 1938, and then only to France). However, the era covered in *Walking in Berlin* was a tumultuous one itself, politically and economically. Evidence of this becomes visible in the book when Hessel visits a warming hall near Alexanderplatz, as well as communist and Nazi rallies, for example. But he is generally not a chronicler of the down-and-out, nor of the outraged. He himself always moved in the circles where fashion, art, and money intersected, and for that reason, *Walking in Berlin* is full of fast cars, socialites, and night life. Like any good snob, it's the middlebrow that truly gives him pause—a trip to a massively popular world-cultures-themed cafe near Potsdamer Platz brings out more bile than our mild-mannered author displays in the entire rest of the book.

Hessel was drawn to French culture and spent significant

portions of his time in France, notably from 1906 to 1913 and again from 1925 to 1927. Among the French concepts that captured his attention was *flâneurie*. He also became an accomplished translator of French literature, and *Walking in Berlin* benefitted from the stylistic skill that he honed on the likes of Balzac, Casanova, and Stendahl. But his most famous translations were the two highly acclaimed volumes of *In Search of Lost Time* that he completed with his close friend Walter Benjamin. The two shared a love of French literature, and together they elevated the concept of the flaneur in German culture. In a review of *Walking in Berlin* entitled 'The Return of the Flaneur', Benjamin celebrated it as 'an absolutely epic book whose source was not memory but rather leisure'.

In her biography of Hessel, Magali Laure Nieradka emphasizes that Hessel was the leader in the relationship: '*The Arcades Project* came into being against the backdrop of Parisian Haussmannisation, *Walking in Berlin* against that of Berlin's modernisation in the 1920s. Nevertheless, *Walking in Berlin* can be viewed as a precursor to *The Arcades Project*, which Hessel had emboldened Benjamin to undertake.' Some lines from Benjamin's *Berlin Childhood Around 1900* are taken nearly word-for-word from *Walking in Berlin*, she notes.[2] The implications of this cultural transfer would resonate through German and international literature and thought, and into our own times.

For all of his literary aspirations and influence, Hessel's approach was a practical one and he hoped that *Walking in*

---

2   Magali Laure Nieradka. *Der Meister der leisen Töne: Biographie des Dichters Franz Hessel*. Oldenburg: Igel Verlag, 2003. p. 112.

Berlin would inspire its readers to inhabit their city differently, to see it with fresh eyes, to make it their own. He even hoped that the residents of Berlin would invent their own word for *flâneurie*, a native word that would imply more leisure than simply 'walking' but that would suit the modern character of the city better than 'promenading'. This specific wish was never fulfilled, but the ongoing interest in his work indicates that the world shares his enthusiasm for exploring Berlin.

The Suspect

Walking slowly down bustling streets is a particular pleasure. Awash in the haste of others, it's a dip in the surf. But my dear fellow citizens of Berlin don't make it easy, no matter how nimbly you weave out of their way. I attract wary glances whenever I try to play the flaneur among the industrious; I believe they take me for a pickpocket.

The swift, firm big-city girls with their insatiably open mouths become indignant when my gaze settles on their sailing shoulders and floating cheeks. That's not to say they have anything against being looked at. But the slow-motion stare of the impassive observer unnerves them. They notice that nothing lies behind my gaze.

No, there's nothing behind it. I simply like to linger at first sight; I'd like to capture and remember these glimpses of the city in which I live …

In the quieter outlying districts, incidentally, I'm no less of a spectacle. There, in the north, is a square with wooden scaffolding, the skeleton of a market, and right beside it, the widow Kohlmann's general store, which also sells rags, and above the bundles of wastepaper, bedsteads, and fur rugs, on the slatted veranda of her shop, there are pots of geraniums. Geraniums — vibrant red in a sluggish grey world — into which

I'm compelled to gaze for a long time.

The widow gives me the evil eye. But she doesn't complain — maybe she thinks I'm an inspector; something's amiss with her papers, for all one knows. But I mean her no harm; I find I'm curious about her business and her views on life. Now she sees I'm finally walking away, as I head toward the cross street, to stare at the backs of the children's knees as they play at hitting a ball against the wall. Long-legged girls — enchanting to watch. They hurl the ball by turns, their hands, heads, and chests twisting as they do so; the hollows of their knees seem to be the centre, and origin, of their movements. Behind me, I feel the widow craning her neck to look. Will she alert the law to this strange fellow's behaviour? Suspicious nature of the observer!

When twilight falls, old and young women lean at the windows, propped up on pillows. I feel for them what psychologists *describe* with words like 'empathy'. But they won't allow me to wait alongside them. I wait alone and for nothing.

Street merchants spruiking their goods don't mind if you linger by them, but I'd rather stand next to the woman with an enormous hairstyle from the previous century, who is slowly spreading her embroidery across blue paper and staring mutely at her customers. And I'm not really one of them; she can hardly expect that I'd buy anything from her.

At times, it is my wont to go into the courtyards. In Berlin, where buildings may be several courtyards deep, life beyond the front dwellings becomes denser and more profound, making the courtyards rich in spirit, those poor courtyards with a bit of green in one corner, the carpet rods, the garbage cans, and the pumps left over from the time before running water. Ideally, I manage to visit them mid-mornings, when singers and violinists emerge, or the organ-grinder man, who also whistles on his free fingers, or the wonder who plays a snare drum on his front and a kettledrum on his back (a cord runs from a hook around his right ankle to the kettledrum behind, up to a pair of cymbals on top; and when he stomps, a mallet strikes the kettledrum, and the cymbals crash together).

Then I stand next to the old porter woman — or rather the doorman's mother, old as she looks, and as accustomed as she seems to sitting on her little camp chair. She takes no offence at my presence, and I'm allowed to look up into the courtyard windows, where young typewriter ladies and sewing girls from the offices and workshops crowd to see the show. They remain, blissfully entranced, until some bothersome boss comes and they have to shuffle back to their work.

The windows are all bare. Only one, on the second-to-top floor, has curtains. A birdcage hangs there, and when the violin cries out, from the depths of its heart, and the barrel organ wails resoundingly, then the canary starts to warble, the only voice from the silently staring windows. It's beautiful. But I also like to spend my share of the evening in these courtyards: the children's last games — they're called to come upstairs, again and again — and the young girls who come home, only to want to leave again. I alone find neither courage nor pretext to intrude; it's too easy to see I'm unauthorised.

Around here, you have to have purpose, otherwise you're

not allowed. Here, you don't walk, you walk *somewhere*. It's not easy for the likes of me.

I count my blessings that, on occasion, a friend takes pity and allows me to accompany her when she has errands to run — to the stocking repair shop, for example, where a sign on the door reads 'Fallen stitches taken up'. In this dreary mezzanine, a hunchback scurries through her musty, wool-laden room, which is brightened by new, glossy wallpaper. Goods and sewing supplies lie atop the tables and étagères, around porcelain slippers, bisque cupids, and bronze statuettes of girls, the way herding animals gather around old fountains and ruins. And I'm allowed to look closely at all of it, and glean a piece of the city's and the world's history from it, while the women confer.

Other times, I'm taken along to a clothing mender who lives on the ground floor of a courtyard building on Kurfürstenstraße. A curtain, which doesn't quite reach the floor, divides his workroom from his sleeping quarters. On a fringed scarf hanging over the curtain, Kaiser Friedrich is colourfully depicted as crown prince. 'That's how he came from San Remo,' the mender says, following my gaze, and then goes on to show me his other monarchist treasures: the last Wilhelm, photographed and very much framed with his daughter on his knees; and the famous picture of the old Kaiser with his children, grandchildren, and great-grandchildren. He says he's 'glad to re-sew my lady-republican's green jacket', but at heart he keeps 'with the old lords', especially as the Republic only cares for the young people. I don't try to convince him otherwise. My understanding of politics is no match for his monarchist objects and objections.

He's always very kind to my friend's dog, which sniffs around at everything, curious and always on the trail of something, just like me. I myself like to go walking with this little terrier. We both get completely lost in thought; and he gives me occasion to stop more often than such a suspicious-looking person as myself would normally be allowed.

Recently, however, things took a bad turn for us. I had gone to pick him up from a building where we were both strangers. We went down a set of stairs in which a grillwork elevator shaft had been installed. The elevator was a grim interloper in the once serenely wide stairwell. From the colourful windows, plump heraldic ladies stared incredulously at this mobile dungeon, and their grips loosened in astonishment around the jewels and emblems in their hands. The smell must have been confusing, with its jumbling of various pasts, distracting my companion to such a degree from our present surroundings and customs that on the first step of the steep staircase, which led down to the foot of the elevator, he *forgot himself!*

Such a thing, my friend later assured me, could only have happened to such a civilised creature in *my* presence. I could tolerate that assertion, but I was harder hit by the accusation made by the building's porter at the moment of the event, who unfortunately stuck his nose out of his box just as we were forgetting ourselves. In proper recognition of my complicity, he turned not to the pup but to me. Pointing with a grey, menacing finger at the site of the misdeed, he barked at me: 'Eh? An' ya wanna be a cultured yuman bein'?'

I Learn a Thing or Two

Yes, he's right. I really must 'culture' myself. Just walking around won't do it. I'll have to educate myself in local history, take an interest in both the past and future of this city, a city that's always on the go, always in the middle of becoming something else. That's what makes it so difficult to pin down, especially for someone who makes his home here ... I think I'll start with the future.

The architect welcomes me into his big, bright atelier and leads me from table to table, showing me plans and plastic models for construction sites, workshops, and office buildings, the laboratories of a rechargeable battery factory, drafts of an aeroplane exhibition hall, drawings for a new residential development that will save thousands of people from housing shortages and the misery of the tenements, raising them up into the air and light. He also tells me about everything Berlin's master builders are planning on doing, or in some cases what they're in the middle of doing. It's not just the city limits and suburbs that they want to transform with big orderly settlements. The new Potsdamer Platz will be surrounded by twelve-storey high-rises. The impoverished Scheunenviertel[1]

---

1   Scheunenviertel: a district in Mitte, in the centre of the city, that was home to a large and impoverished eastern European Jewish population at the time.

will disappear. Around Bülowplatz[2] and Alexanderplatz, a new world will appear in massive city blocks. New projects are constantly being developed to solve the problems of real estate and traffic. In the future, neither the speculator nor the architect will be allowed to mar the city's style with their single edifices. Our building codes won't permit that.

The architect describes his colleagues' ideas: since the city will gradually reach one of the banks of the Havel River in Potsdam, one of them draws up a plan with train lines and arterial roads in which he includes the lovely wooded areas and scattered lakes, ultimately incorporating them as Hamburg has done. Another colleague wants to build a large imposing square between the Brandenburg Gate and Tiergarten, so that the Siegesallee[3] that now cuts through the park would mark its limit. On the fairgrounds, the exhibition centre would be shaped like a gigantic egg, with inner and outer rings of halls, a new athletic forum, and a canal with a waterside restaurant between garden terraces. The Potsdamer and Anhalter train stations would be relocated to a sidetrack of a suburban train line to make room for a broad avenue with department stores, hotels, and parking garages. With the completion of the Midland Canal,[4] Berlin's network of waterways is changing, and the corresponding renovation and construction of riverbanks,

2 Bülowplatz is known as Rosa-Luxemburg-Platz today.

3 At the time a large boulevard through the middle of Tiergarten, Siegesallee was later razed as part of Albert Speer's National Socialist plan to redevelop the city.

4 The Midland Canal (Mittellandkanal) is Germany's longest man-made waterway, linking France, Switzerland, Poland, the Czech Republic, and the Baltic Sea; begun 1906 and extended until 1938.

bridges, and facilities is a significant challenge. And then there are the new building materials: glass and concrete. People now use glass instead of bricks and marble. There are already a number of houses whose floors and stairs are made of black glass, and their walls are made of opaque glass or alabaster. And there are iron buildings, clad in ceramic and framed in gleaming bronze.

The architect notices my bewilderment with a smile. So he gives me a quick demonstration. Down to the street and into his waiting car. We hurtle down Kurfürstendamm, past old architectural horrors and new 'solutions' and redemptions. We stop in front of the cabaret and the movie palace, which form such an emphatic unit precisely because of their quiet dissimilarities, both wheeling cheerily through the air, constantly tracing the stirring simplicity of their own lines, though the one is short and squat while the other towers over it. The master next to me explains the work of masters. And in order to illustrate what he is describing, he gets out of the car, leads me down a deep twilight-red passageway into one of the theatre's auditoriums, and shows me how the entire room is circular, and that the walls are covered in an uninterrupted expanse of patterned wallpaper.

Then we drive down a cross street through a middle-class bit of Charlottenburg, past Lake Lietzen, to the radio tower and exhibition halls, which he expands to larger fairgrounds with a few words. Before he'd finished, we reached Reichskanzlerplatz[5],

---

5   Reichskanzlerplatz: known as Theodor-Heuss-Platz today, after being renamed 'Adolf-Hitler-Platz' under National Socialism.

and he describes an entertainment centre that is planned here, both blocks full of cinemas, restaurants, dance halls, a big hotel, and a tower of lights that would soar over all of it. We turn onto a street parallel to Kaiserdamm and stop in front of a vast new development. My guide himself is the building contractor here. Foremen approach us and debrief him. Meanwhile, I gaze into the rambling chaos at the two pillars of the entryway, already clearly recognisable even in their bare brickwork. Then I walk with the master, over detritus and debris, to the edge of the site, beyond which the abyss of the middle yawns. The floor plan, which one must normally read from the notation of 'frozen music' on a drawing table, now lays spread out before me. Here are the two large depots where the train cars will bed down. Tracks will stretch out *this* way. All around the edges, gardens will emerge where children of the officials, drivers, and conductors will play beneath the windows of the many bright apartments. We drive along one edge of the big rectangle. At one point, the street is just coming into being and plants run riot over our path. And all around us, a whole city grows from the contractor's words.

After making so many unfinished things visible to me, he can now show me things in their completion. Our car hurries across the bridge over the Spree River near the Charlottenburg Palace and along the canal to far-flung Westhafen. A glance at the grim Plötzensee Prison walls. From the endless Seestraße, we reach the churchyard wall and the tenements, and then Müllerstraße. A terrific assembly of train cars and people appears. The horizon clears as we approach, allowing us a view of three halls supported by iron framework.[6] We stride through the entryway and, from within the courtyard, we observe the three-storey wings of the apartment buildings, the four-storey front building, the hulking pillars in the corners. Then we poke around everywhere, first in the glass-and-iron hall where the train cars are housed. We gaze up at the train-station dome, and down into the strange world of the walkways and rails. Then the administrative offices, then the repair shops, and finally up an inviting flight of stairs into one of the lovely apartments.

While walking around the complex, I comprehend, without being able to express myself in the proper structural engineering terms, how its creator was able to lend this enormous brick thing — which must be a train station, office, and home all at once — an unforgettably unified character by repeating certain motifs, emphasising certain lines; by bringing forward sharp edges on the rising surfaces and other such elements.

On the north-eastern side, we gaze across fields and into the distance, at the giant building's tiny neighbour, a little house 'so wind-worried', as the poem[7] goes, standing far afield. People call it 'the shrimp'. The juxtaposition of these towering halls and that hut is like an emblem of the silhouette of Berlin.

* * *

In the evening of that overfilled day, I was welcomed into the home of an elderly lady who produced keepsakes from her chests and escritoire, things that had once belonged to her

---

6   Hessel is describing the Seestraße train depot.

7   'Der Knabe und das Immlein' by Eduard Friedrich Mörike.

forebears in an old house on Stralauerstraße: a big English doll in a greyed muslin empire dress and still-pink silk shoes with ribbons bound about her ankles in a crisscross pattern; little plates and candlesticks of carefully carved wood that these forebears played with as children in the garden near the Spree River and the wooden Waisen Bridge,[8] where Chodowiecki[9] gazes into the water in Menzel's[10] famous painting. The elderly lady removes, from a tin, home-ownership documents with wax seals. She allows me to open fragile family registers belonging to her great-grand-aunts, in which poetic dedications in hair-fine, flourishing script stand opposite to tinted bouquets, and delicate landscapes by artist friends. The landscapes are ornamented here and there with horsemen in yellow frocks and bucket-top boots, or an equestrienne in violet dress. The form and colour of the bouquets is kindred to that on the plates and vases and bowls at the Royal Porcelain Factory Berlin.

She even places a bridal crown from the year 1765 in my hands: flower-shaped wire braided with green silk. I'm allowed to touch an agate tobacco tin. The gracious owner of all of these treasures takes small family portraits down from the walls: female heads with curling, lightly powdered hair and daintily tinged scarves, men in wigs with dark-blue frocks. And then she tells me about the Berliner parlours, the more

---

8   Waisen Bridge (Orphan Bridge): so named because of its proximity to an orphanage, the wooden bridge was replaced with a stone one in 1894 as part of efforts to make Berlin a more suitable royal seat.

9   Daniel Niklaus Chodowiecki, a Polish-German painter and etcher, lived in Berlin; director of the Berlin Academy of Art.

10 Adolph Friedrich Erdmann von Menzel (1815 – 1905), a 19th-century German artist.

beautiful predecessors to the 'front rooms' with mahogany furniture and the blue and red salons that our grandparents had. These parlours were shuttered sanctums in which children could only set foot on special occasions. We open up one of her favourite books, *Childhood Memories of an Old Berliner* by Felix Eberty,[11] and read:

> The walls were painted light-grey. Only the wealthiest people had carpets. As a wedding present, Wilhelm Schadow, a boyhood friend of my father's who would later become director of the Kunstakademie Düsseldorf, had painted a beautiful, vivid rendition of the four seasons, grey-on-grey accented with white highlights, so that it seemed as if they were in relief. An exquisite carpet woven with strawberry leaves, flowers, and fruit covered the floor and the furniture was delicately fashioned of white birch wood. A small chandelier of four lights hanging on beaded glass chains seemed exceedingly sumptuous to us, an untouchable work of art, which we would have all-too-well liked to hold in our hands, if it hadn't been strictly forbidden; the possibility of satisfying this desire was within reach, because the height of the ceiling would have allowed us to touch the gleaming glass morsels with the aid of a chair.

We speak of even older Berlin interiors. She has paintings of rooms where *l'hombre* tables[12] stand decked in needlework,

---

11 *Jugenderinnerungen eines alten Berliners*. Berlin: 1878.

12 A *l'hombre* table is a three-sided table made specifically for playing the card game of the same name, the popularity of which peaked around the beginning of the 1700s.

with embroidered sofas, the servants with the prettily painted porcelain cups, an English repeater[13] on the bureau, a 'well-conditioned' varnished grand piano from the Frederician era in the corner. She remembers the high beds that were accessed by a series of steps, canopy beds *à la duchess*[14] as well as *à tombeau*,[15] canopy rope and fringe, nightdress and gloves, hand-designed tapestries with figures in the French style. She produces an endless supply of possessions: daguerreotypes, copperplate engravings daubed in India ink, cut-out figures …

A bronze flower-basket hangs over us, green-glass leaves and pale glass morning glories spilling over the top. This item is from the thirties or the forties of the previous century, when a new relish for Rococo sprang up. The light flickers in the night wind as if it weren't electrical, but rather the light of an oil lamp. It's late for old ladies. And I realise how tired I am from so much Berlin.

---

13 A repeater is a type of watch or clock that chimes the hour (and sometimes the quarter hour) at the push of a button; popular before electrical lighting, as the time could be read in the dark.

14 Canopy bed *à la duchess*: a bed whose canopy posts are not visible.

15 Canopy bed *à tombeau:* a bed whose posts are taller at the head than at the foot, resulting in a sloping canopy, often hung with thick draperies; also known as a tent or field bed.

A Bit of Work

It's true that other cities display more lust for life, enjoyment, and diversion than Berlin does. Maybe *their* inhabitants understand how to entertain themselves in a way that is at once more natural and more cultivated. Their pleasures are both more visible and more beautiful. But Berlin has its own particular and visible beauty, whenever and wherever it is at work. You have to go looking for it in its temples of machinery, in its churches of precision. There is no lovelier building than that monumental hall of glass and reinforced concrete: the Peter Behrens turbine factory[1] on Huttenstraße. And no cathedral offers a more impressive view than the galleries of this hall, upon which you are eye-to-eye with the man whose aerial crane transports heavy loads of iron. Even before you understand just how the metal monsters down below produce further monstrosities, you're smitten by the mere sight of them: castings and housings, unassembled barrel cogs and wheel-shafts, pumps and half-completed generators, jig-boring mills and gear racks ready for installation, giant and dwarf machines in testing, and parts of turbo-generators in the concrete-paved spin pit.

Though we're more awed than informed in this hall, a few things become more accessible to us in the little workshop. We

---

1   The AEG turbine factory, still standing today at Huttenstraße 12–19.

see rods of nickel steel being milled and ground on a blade, sheet-metal teeth sliding into the grooves of an inductor shaft, coiled spools reaching between the teeth. We visit the forge, where the workers hold glowing bars of iron under the steam hammer, which dents and cleaves them like wax.

We stand by the water in front of the transformer factory, watching how coal is transported, with a beam hoist trolley, from a barge on the Spree into a trip-hammer mill, so that it can all be pulverised without the touch of a human hand. We enter the hall, where no one else is present, and observe the combustion in the smouldering grotto. After the halls with the big machines, we visit the rooms where female workers spool very fine wire, and roll laminated paper and press it into layers of very light, hard, smooth cylinders. They pass around a little punch plate. They anneal,[2] oil, and trim.

In the meter factory, one motion of the machine turns sheet metal into bowls with upturned rims, and a second motion punches a hole in them. They're riveted and soldered in a shower of sparks. Magnets are inserted. The whole building is a chain of work, which meanders uninterrupted over the workbenches, from floor to floor, the goods shoved down chutes for further processing. All of the parts, and parts of parts, that the seated women lay hand on are integrated into the emerging meter, joined, screwed in, and tested; and finally the whole construction is packaged. Steel bands are wrapped around boxes, which are pushed on rollers to the elevator; no human hand touches them there, but, rather, they are lifted with

---

2   Annealing is a heat process that makes a metal more workable and ductile.

a lever. All waste of effort and exertion is avoided; increasingly, the workers are merely the custodians and controllers of machines. The girls put their mugs for tea, coffee, or cocoa on the conveyor belts, which return from their circuit through the kitchen heated and ready. Each girl sitting there has only a little plot of table for herself behind the conveyor belt, but it's room enough for a birthday celebration's brightly coloured cups, plates, and spoons. They make a touching still-life behind the moving marvel of engineering.

It's still not necessary to understand everything; you just have to see for yourself how things are perpetually happening and transforming. At one of these reverent shrines of fervour, it's said there's a metal that has a particularly high melting point and is very difficult to vaporise. It can't be melted in ovens — they would go to pieces — so it must be gradually crushed, sintered, hammered, and annealed into a solid bar, which can then be formed into wire. And now you can watch the wire pass through the hammering machine and draw plate, tapered and annealed and pulled until it is a hair-fine filament that will be used in a light bulb. Machines do all of that. The people just turn things on, take things out, push them down the line. And while a thousand thin and ever-thinner wires come into being, in other rooms a thousand bulbs grow. Patient operators sit at revolving machining tables that turn before their very hands, placing the caps and removing them again, and the machine obediently crimps the foot of the bulb, inserts a bracket, tightens the mounting, fuses, vacuum seals, caps off, solders, etches, stamps, and packs. But once again that's just part of the work: there's still testing and measuring and sorting to do, finishing and dyeing.

All of that takes place ceaselessly in Siemensstadt, Charlottenburg, Moabit, Gesundbrunnen, and beyond the Warschauer Bridge and along the upper Spree.

And it's so fantastic to look down into the hall, from the stairs or the gallery, at the whirring, gyrating machines; so gripping is the view of the necks and hands of those pottering about there, and when their upward-glancing eyes meet your own.

The things these people make fill your little room with light — a light that wanders from house to house, illuminates, extols, advertises, and outlines. Luminescent fluting on the ceiling of an enormous room forms a festive tent of light. Contour lighting articulates a building's facade, floodlights saturate window displays, blue daylight lamps glow in a hall of silks, and the fabric that the salesman presents has the same colour it would under the sun. Outside, electric writing scrolls across signs, letters form words and disappear, pictures appear and change, colourful wheels roll silently.

Whole buildings now exist with a structure based on light. One can conjecture the department store of the future, whose walls and ceilings will be glass. The whole thing will be one enormous brightness: in day, the down-rushing sun all around; at night, the man-and-machine-made light.

That's what the great halls of iron and electricity are working toward; but to really grasp Berlin's industriousness, you also need to take a walk through the smaller factories. You have to set foot in one of the building complexes and courtyards of the southeast. Visit, as I did, the frame factory in the luxury-goods and leather quarter. The wood is stored on the floor just as it came from the sawmill, drying in the light breeze. When it's cut to size, every plank keeps a strip of bark from its forest home along its edge. Then it goes into a notching machine with fine teeth that bite into the corners to dovetail the pieces of the frame, and the chippings fly out of the exhaust ducts. The long slats are hewn with a circular saw. If the men in the great machine halls appear small next to their colossi, like seamen or miners next to elemental forces, here they tame their machine-animals with a ringmaster's glance. My eyes are drawn to the hunched gent there at the circular saw, who grimaces imperiously each time the blade tears into the wood under his hand.

Many girls and women are stationed near the bubbling pots of paste, and by the glass and cardboard that is inserted into the frames. The paste girls are a coarser sort than the glue girls or polishers. And you could conduct a study on the relationship between the motions required for these activities, and the hand that executes them. What fine fingers has the girl who pushes fine little nails into the layer of cardboard behind the frames. How patient are the long hands of the woman who trims the edges of the frame to fit behind the glass. How childishly round are the hands of the bright blonde who presses a tin mould into a chalky mass, and slips the moistened form onto a wooden board, just as children do with sand in a playground. Her work is an agreeable specialisation, because the rococo ornaments she adds to the frames aren't as in demand as the straight ones;

they're more expensive to produce and not as modern. That lends them and their oblivious creator a particular beauty. The gilders work in separate rooms. They have gas masks on their faces for the bronze dust, which is dangerous for the lungs. Unfortunately, the public only wants — and therefore the many little shops that sell oil paintings only want — golden frames. After the days of inflation, the Germans once again need a bit of glitter in their hovels. Even frames for photographs must be gilded. Good old mahogany is no longer wanted. Someone tells me another historically interesting tidbit about the photograph frames: assemblage frames used to be popular, the kind you could put multiple pictures in, a whole clan. Now, they'd rather display each picture individually. And so we move from the frames to the framed: the kindly manager of the factory leads me into the showroom for the most popular oil prints. It's very instructive. For among not-exactly-essential objects — however one chooses to label luxury items or staples of popular spiritual sustenance — the oil print plays a large role. It furnishes an infinite number of rooms and souls.

For years, the industry 'bestseller' has remained the holy penitent Mary Magdalene, who lounges softly in her blue robes, gazing in coquettish contemplation at a skull. She seems to be coveted not only by the pious, as is the case with other reproductions from the realm of Bible stories and legends; the worldly also want her. Lounging, lightly clad women are odds-on favourites anyway. Their cupid-bedecked 'divans', dissolving in cloaks of clouds, are often framed not in an upright format, but rather a wide one that makes a nice impression over the bed. Should the young couples who buy such idyllic prints have serious designs for offspring, the beauty in the painting straightens herself a bit and watches over one or more children. Pets are also welcomed, to make the familial harmony even more complete. A contemporary adjustment was recently made to one of the most popular of these ladies, my seasoned guide recounts: at the audience's request, her rich head of curls had to be removed in favour of a bob. In other respects, the customer remains traditional: the notorious painting *Beethoven* — in which a group of men and women draped across or crouched upon twilit divans listen to a piano — hasn't yet made room for a jazz band. The President of the Reich doesn't enjoy much popularity among men of importance now that he's a civilian; and the average German family already stocked up on portraits of him in military tunics during the war.

The seasons, with their beloved labours and pleasures — sowers, grain binders, and hunters in their corresponding landscapes — are always easy to 'move', and each especially in its given time. That surprises me a little, as I would have thought spring would be coveted in winter, and summer in autumn.

I'm beginning to develop an interest in statistics. I'd like to determine more precisely: how many Mary Magdalenes does Magdeburg need? How many ladies on divans does Wrocław demand? In what areas does good old Arnold Böcklin's[3] *Silence of the Forest* outstrip everything else? How has Munich's taste for

---

3   Arnold Böcklin (1827–1901) was a Swiss symbolist painter, wildly popular at
     the time. Nabokov noted that prints of his *Isle of the Dead* were to be 'found in
     every Berlin home'.

oil prints changed from 1918 to 1928? In which provinces and cities does the demand for lady with child, children, or animals outweigh that for lady with cupids alone? Yes, I'm beginning to develop an interest in statistics.

* * *

As the market of Baghdad has its bazaars, so Berlin has districts for its various enterprises. Spittelmarkt, I'm told, separates the ready-to-wear clothing quarter from the coat-making. I visit a hat factory on the ready-to-wear side, where I'm brought to the drafters who cut shapes out of cardboard based on Parisian models, then to the girls who cut these shapes from cloth and leather, into the humming hall of the seamstresses, and finally into a room where iron moulds are heated with electricity. It's there that the hats, now sewn and shaped, take on their final form. They're treated with steam from a hose, then put in a sort of oven, where they braise on in silence. For the cultural historian, it's not insignificant that hatbands are completely out, but the finishing often imitates the shape of a ribbon or bandeau. Nor is the fact that since scanty berets have come into vogue, many caps have been made which are not quite as austere as a beret, but are somewhat wider, like a squire's hat. In this factory, where a hat ordered this morning will be delivered this evening, nearly everything is created in-house, from drawing table to packaging. Only a small proportion of the hats are ordered from the so-called workshops, which operate as a cottage industry.

I'm informed about the significant role that this division of labour typically plays in the Berlin ready-to-wear business, in

which 'overseers' from the large companies take fabric based on
the pattern of the collection, and have part of it handled by their
own employees, and part by women working from home. Such
overseers work for the big apron factory, for example, which I
visit in one of the enormous courtyards of Köpenickerstraße.
It has its own building in Vogtland where the material is
manufactured. Here, the material is fed into machines that cut
many layers at once; it's fed into industrious hands that use
their little machines to place a hem-stitch or three pleats or
to sew on buttons that are fixed more firmly than those sewn
by human hands. At this enterprise, I'm also allowed to enter
the offices and get acquainted with the new enhancements to
the sales department. I see computing machines that multiply,
machines for postage and labelling, new-fangled card-index
files, and, on the wall, maps with the itineraries of travelling
salesmen, for whom two-score sample cases stand waiting in
large automobiles in the garage down below.

An entire study could be conducted on the arrangement of
Berlin's 'bazaars'. Besides the large carpentry and metalworking
districts, cottage industries, wool wares and ready-to-wear areas,
there are other specialties: for example, a street where lighting
fixtures have been manufactured for many decades, Ritterstraße.
On Moritzplatz, you'll find the international-export warehouses
for items that come from the Ore Mountains, Thuringia, and
North Bohemia, such as rocking horses, doll tea-cosies, combs,
Jesus figurines, tin soldiers, and rubber horsemen. All along
Seydelstraße, busts and wax heads stand eerily in the display
windows. Thousands of dummies — 'stylistic devices', if you

will, of the 'art of window dressing' — overrun Germany and beyond, wearing shirts, dresses, jackets, and hats. It's interesting the sorts of faces the wax-headed mannequins make! They challenge you with pursed lips, they squint, and their gaze drips out like poison. Their cheeks aren't milk and blood, but rather sallow yellow-grey with green-gold shadows. No hydrogen peroxide can induce such a brutal blond as their hair. Often their faces have only a rough form, and then their implied expressions are particularly perverse. Taken together, their stiffness and their elasticity expresses a cool mixture of insolence and distinction, which you, you poor thing, won't be able to resist. Their stages of undress are thrilling. The gold-naked ones shine and the silver ones gleam, wearing nothing but brownish shoes; bare-breasted ones sport a sort of loincloth and stockings in order to spare you their complete nakedness. The men's heads are also interesting. It's remarkable how many of these 'men of action' wear determined expressions and tiny glued-on moustaches. If they have bodies, and not just a puppet's stand, they must be shrouded in black jerseys, unless they're sauntering in evening attire, complete with smoking jacket, among the naked ladies, all while gazing over the heads of children in little blue dresses and flattering red ties, who caper about before us. But in the courtyard of busts, there are also individual legs. And puzzling frameworks: for example, a golden ball, above which a female torso ends in one stylised arm and one cut-off stump. Surely all of this has a reasonable explanation, but I stare, ignorant, at the abundance of beings and parts of them, frames and faces — some of which even wear glasses.

Fashion

There are notices in the papers: 'An enormous collection of enchanting evening gowns in all of the latest colours' or 'MEINE rock-bottom clearance sale for fur-trimmed coats' with the name and address of a company someplace in the east. We're curious to see it (and by 'we', I mean the woman who told me about all this), and we end up at shops in the most calamitous courtyards, not a hint of glamour about. And we find ourselves in an environment that is as favourable to buying and selling as that of the Parisian emporiums. Though no boss or floor manager here knows a woman's heart's desire as they do in Paris, calling out to the hesitant shopper with a friendly 'Fouillez, Madame,' the same principle is in effect: to open the floodgates of unchecked caressing, until it becomes the sort of lust that deprives all ladies of reason and fills the tills to overflowing. With prices clearly marked, there are crumpled lace dresses, frippery-bespangled muslins, dingy velvet capes with collars made of some unidentifiable fur — cheap, sordid 'finery'. Flowers throng in cardboard boxes, while tabletops are crowded with jewellery whose selling point is that its damage is hardly noticeable. Tall stacks of invitingly tangled pink and purple undergarments, richly embellished with lace, look luxurious from a distance. Next to them are evening shoes with clasps made of diamond and emerald. This overstock and liquidation bazaar is not only for casual and professional 'coquettes'. Sensible articles are also mixed in among the false finery: coarse bedsheets and stout leather boots, bedside rugs and sheer curtains whose prices, though not reduced, still aren't to be beat.

We visit next a department store, the name of which is also known throughout west Berlin. It radiates the promise of the lucky find, which women react to, and which excites them, even if nothing more is at stake than half a dozen towels or a pair of warm gloves. And the only other stores nearby are boring ones, with lifeless displays that suggest nothing more than the exchange of wares and money. There's nothing to awaken our interest until we're standing before the incandescent brightness of the gigantic department-store complex. Though it's not so crowded, so cavalierly artistic, so cunningly opulent as the place we just left, we still enjoy the variety presented by the orderly abundance of wares. Our needs, which just a moment ago seemed so formidable to us, suddenly seem Lilliputian in scale. But we can be helped. The salespeople have studied 'serving the customer' from the ground up. The great department stores have created schools in which the teachers, who are educated at universities of commerce, give the girls an object lesson in the treatment of wares and customers. We have only the faintest inkling who we are dealing with when the little ladies of Wertheim and Tietz[1] suavely make their rounds, trained in the art of sales and suggestion.

---

1   Two large department store chains.

Berlin's great department stores are neatly arranged theatres of tremendous organisation. And they pamper their visitors with a high level of convenience. Should you buy a metre-long pink-rubber strap from a revolving stand made of glittering brass, your gaze will rest on marble, and glide along mirrors and the gleaming parquetry floor while your wares are registered in a notepad. We sit on granite benches in atriums and winter gardens, our packages on our laps. Art exhibitions spill into tearooms and infringe on the toy and bathroom departments. We wander under decorative canopies of velvet and silk to the soaps and toothbrushes. Strange how little these grand department stores, which are dedicated to the masses, take the masses' need for kitsch into account. Many of the objects on offer are nearly sensible. Popular taste cannot resist the adjective 'respectable'.

Only in the storehouses of sewing goods and fashion accessories does one stumble across an accumulation of dubious items. In the ready-to-wear storehouses, one finds only sedate, inconspicuous clothing that approaches fashion hesitantly, with resistance, trying to disguise it rather than making any concessions. This ready-to-wear precinct feels a little empty, as if a more thoughtful element is missing. The stacks of pots and baking pans, the curtain rings and breakfast services, seem particularly bright and cheerful.

Nearby, one of Berlin's most celebrated fashion houses occupies the length of three buildings. Models draw in a large audience. Fashion-minded ladies from all — except the most exclusive — circles sit at delicately decorated tables as the lovely models sidle by. They tread forth in festive little gossamer dresses to the tones of a chorus, and smile as their profession demands, so that you can tell them apart from those other ladies, who arrive later or leave earlier.

This boutique, with its not unjustified pretension, is an extended outlier of fashion, whose zone really begins where the city centre and the old west touch. Its many displays take their rightful place on Leipziger Straße and Friedrichstraße, often one after the next. But it's only after you've left the storefronts of the Wertheim department store behind you, along with the Potsdamer Platz hotel block, and turn onto Bellevuestraße or Friedrich-Ebertstraße, that you approach its headquarters, on Lennéstraße, on the fringe of the Tiergarten. Fashion lives … in a house with a garden.

The golden letters of the name that spells 'taste' flicker through the green of the garden. In the late morning and early afternoon, you see lines of cars there, carefully polished, very 'racy', driven right out of the catalogues of their manufacturers, brand-sparkling-new and flawless. Dour chauffeurs await their 'esteemed lady'. These ladies are greeted so submissively by the saleswomen that one might think that the tides of absolute monarchy had not yet ebbed. They are led past rococo armchairs, over flowered carpets, into the salon — the boss hurries by — and 'small talk' about the weather, travel, and health is conducted while the models step up to show the customer their next change of style. The boss usually appears dissatisfied. He tugs at bows, rearranges a belt, shakes his head doubtfully. Seldom does one see a rapturous smile, like those on the faces of the saleswomen in Paris department stores, who know how to communicate their unwavering approval. But the 'dressed' Berlin lady doesn't seem perturbed by the boss's behaviour. 'You know what suits me', is a phrase he hears not as flattery but as an exhortation. More importantly, he knows what suits them better than they do. Why, he saw the collections of the most important fashion designers in Paris on the models at the *défilé*, and made his selections with Frau von X and Frau Z in mind. There aren't really all that many options in that regard. The image of Berlin's society woman will remain uniform for as long as she is reliant on the selection of clothing that is placed in front of her as the *'crème'* of French production. Again and again, the fatal coincidence comes to pass: three or four ladies meet wearing the same dress. Is it any consolation that they all possess the 'hit' of the season?

From the standpoint of society, Berlin is still small, and the elegance of its ladies is a second-hand product. But a new type of woman is emerging, victorious over those whose tailor and milliner live next to the Tiergarten: the young avant-gardiste, the post-war Berlin woman. The years around 1910 must have been a particularly good vintage. They produced girls with lightly athletic shoulders. They walk so lovely and weightlessly in their dresses, and their skin is superb — makeup only illuminates it. Their healthy smiles and the confidence with which they force their way in pairs through the afternoon melee on Tauentzienstraße and Kurfürstendamm are refreshing. No, 'force' isn't the right word. They do the crawl when everyone else is doing the breaststroke. Sharp and smooth, they steer up to the window displays. Where on earth did they get their pretty dresses, their hats and coats?

Along with the big department stores that have already been mentioned here, in the Bavarian Quarter near Kurfürstenstraße, on a side street of Kurfürstendamm, there are many smaller fashion boutiques. They mostly make do with a first name as their *enseigne*. They also have a Parisian role model or two. *Vogue* and *Femina* are laid out; *Harper's Bazaar* and *Art, Goût et Beauté*. The owner of the shop has a light touch, and her customers know their own bodies precisely. These youths are beginning to discover a style that is neither the snobbishness of the 'brands' nor the indifference that can be satisfied with mass production. Is it already true, as we hear ever more loudly, that in terms of elegance the Berlin woman can measure herself among the best in Europe? We wouldn't want to do any petty auditing of the situation. We should be satisfied to watch these droves of young and very young girls — this *défilé* of youth and freshness in slim, well-fitted dresses, with little hats from which a lock of hair has freed itself, their long legs' elastic stride — to be convinced that Berlin is well on its way to becoming an elegant city.

Lust for Life

These young people are also learning how to enjoy things, which doesn't come naturally to Germans. In his zeal for pleasure, the Berliner of yesterday still lapses into the dangers of accumulation, quantity, excess. His coffee houses are establishments of pretentious refinement. Nowhere to be found are the cosy, unremarkable leather sofas, the quiet corners, so loved by the Parisians and the Viennese. Instead of saying 'waiter', the Berliner still calls after the stupidly titled *Herr Ober*, simple ground coffee is called a *mokka double*, fifty barmaids at the counter are greater than ten. New 'Grand Cafés' are always being established, with room for around a thousand guests. On the ground floor, there's a Hungarian ensemble; on the second floor, two bands entertain the dancers. 'Peculiar' lady orators take the stage. The ads and notices promise international attractions, a cosmopolitan establishment, etc. Yes, you surely do get something for your money. 'With free entry and 3 marks' purchase you'll enjoy Germany's best cabaret uninterrupted from 8.30 to 12.30. Afternoon refreshment 2 marks 50 with cake, as much as you'd like.'

Business, business! Even the old-fashioned souls want to experience it.

Once in your life, you must experience the day after

Christmas in one of these monster establishments, when all and sundry go out, and the help has the day off. Then Daddy really has deep pockets — though a lot can be had for pretty cheap. There are mixed platters of hors d'oeuvres with everything included: lobster and caviar and artichoke hearts, and all of it always for two people — double portions, like the gigantic *entrecôte* garnished with just a side of vegetables. There are first-class dessert platters. Nothing is lacking. Of course the son, sitting quietly bored next to his scantily clad mother, already knows that it's more sophisticated to order something lavish, and perhaps he'll impress his elders with his special selection. He's more nonchalant toward the waiter than his father is. He'd rather be sitting over by those two unaccompanied young ladies. They may well be typists, going out alone today in spite of the men. They order very tastefully: French vegetable platters, *chicorée* and *laitue braisée*, only cocktails as an accompaniment, and afterwards table water with their meringues. He glances across at them and takes note. The back of his head is shaved in the American style, but there's no roll of fat back there like his father has …

The monstrous double concerts that the capital city puts on for the tongue, eye, ear, and dancing foot entice the new youth, our new Berlin girls. As far as eating, drinking, and smoking go, they have a few new methods — amusing dietary restrictions and stringent exercise habits. They steer themselves through the crush of pleasures as assuredly as they steer through the streets, finding a few paths for dancing among the thick of human masses. They know which hotels and locales you can dance at in the afternoon if need be, and they have their cocktail parties where one dances in private company. It's admirable how they master Berlin's *Karneval*, which notoriously doesn't end with Shrove Tuesday and Ash Wednesday, but goes on for weeks, uninterrupted. And there are nights with three or more important parties: one in the halls of the 'Zoo', one at the Kroll Opera House, one in the Akademie zu Charlottenburg, one in the Philharmonie, and, on top of them, a more intimate and particularly tantalising one in this atelier or that. They know how to pick them, they know where the best band is playing, they create clever itineraries in order to accomplish more. Above all else, they're out for good dancing. Having the right dance partner is very important, and this figure is not to be confused with whomever you love at the moment. *His* task is a completely different one. My young lady friends have informed me on this point while putting themselves together for one party or another. This preparation, this *Débarquement pour Cythère*, is a significant moment, and for us observers, it is sometimes more instructive than the party itself. You should see their earnest expressions in the mirror as they bronze their arms and shoulders, make up their faces, try on turbans and feathered caps. They don't rush; they carefully add the final touches to the evening's work, like an artist who wants to create something lasting. They invent wonderful forms midway between a masquerade costume and an evening dress: innocent bare flesh, enticing concealments, and grotesque exaggerations in which to hide themselves away.

Meanwhile, you can enjoy their presence in peace, which otherwise isn't easy; they generally keep the same rhythm as their Berlin, which leaves the likes of *us* somewhat breathless. It's astounding how many places and people they can dispatch in an evening without growing weary. 'Now let's go have an aperitif,' they say suddenly, when tea-time has grown a bit too meditative. 'Aperitif?' I ask, bewildered. 'I thought that didn't exist in this country.' 'Once again you underestimate our city's spirit,' I'm scolded. And before I know it, I'm sitting in the car next to the quickest of them as she drives down Budapester Straße, past the glass atriums where the 'smartest' domestic and foreign cars are on display, and stops across from the dinosaurs that are chiselled into the walls of the aquarium. We traipse over the glass plate at the entrance to the hotel, a glowing plate with a paradisiacal inscription. In the foyer, Maria (she demands that her friends call her that, to spite the laughable Marys, Miezes, and Mias of her set) exchanges a few words with a young poet who will soon appear in a film, and inquires after the health of their mutual friend, a boxer who's been out of the game for a long time. The boy who hurries up to them with a message, posthaste, is the newest star of the cabaret. Maria cuts things short and pulls me on. In the lobby of the bar, the exedra so to speak, groups of men converse on sofas lining the walls, and if I were better informed, I would recognise certain politicians or stockbrokers. We step into a pleasant lower room with red ceiling beams. We had hoped to take our places on the high stools at the bar, but they're all occupied. And so Maria has to inform me from our table who the slim man in the nice sand-coloured shirt speaking English at the next table is, and who his companion with the side-whiskers is. Maria is greeted by the young attaché's table. And the sweet creature she swiftly kissed while brushing past, that was the new wonder of the revue, whom I recognise from pictures in the magazines. Two girls sit right next to us, both a little too freshly painted. Maria thinks she saw the one on the right in St. Moritz. 'And why is the one on the left wrinkling her nose for the second time?' 'One does that a great deal now. [She names an actress] did it on the stage. It's in vogue.'

Around the tables, whispers fly like in the best of Europe. That is, in the new Berlin one doesn't speak as loudly as in the old one. It's as if you're at a reception here. But Maria doesn't allow more than a quarter-hour's visit. She has a date for an early dinner at the Neva Grill with friends who want to go to the 'Komödie' afterwards. She hands me over to one of her friends, who is supposed to take me to Restaurant Horcher. That's where Maria wants to meet us in an hour. 'You can eat and drink Burgundy there with manly languor and distinction. I'll make it for dessert.'

The sole, which my companion, Gert, had decided upon for me following a consultation with the son of the house, was prepared before our eyes in the good Parisian fashion. Over a Nuits-Saint-Georges, I let Gert, who, although young, was already respected in banking and diplomatic circles, tell me about Berlin society. It's a concept that's both hard to grasp and to define. The old divisions between the estates are ever crumbling. Of course, there are still a few ill-humoured nobles in Potsdam and on country estates, mourning for the heyday of exclusive court society. But it's precisely the most genteel among them who seek to connect with the new times. Hospitable houses unify art and the haute bourgeoisie, and at the tables of great bank barons, socialist delegates meet with princes of former ruling houses. The big athletic clubs have established a new attitude, which does away with the heel-clicking of former guard lieutenants and the gallantry of the old students' corps. With youthful enthusiasm, the ambitious Berliner plunges into this new conviviality, and our ministers and secretaries have to attend more strategic dinners than is ultimately good for politics. We come to the topic of women, and just as Gert was telling of a dinner party where he sat between two of them — the one on the right wanting to be discreetly and properly entertained, while the one on the left tried to make a double entendre in every second remark, and brought up topics that would have made our mothers blanch with shame — in walked Maria, seeming like the young queen of a new nation of Amazons, for whom the old 'society' no longer existed. She isn't interested in continuing our discussion; she just wants to pick us up in time to get to an important Russian film. Gert really wants to see the one by the Parisian-American that was made using only a few objects from the studio, shirt collars, and hands. But Maria already saw that one on her last stay in Paris, in a small theatre at the Ursulines in the Latin Quarter.

After the cinema, we sit downstairs in the Casanova, not far from the piano, where a composer plays his hit song nightly and sings. Gert and Maria deliberate on what else we could do. 'Why don't you young people go upstairs and dance?' I ask. 'I don't want to,' says Maria, 'but maybe Gert would find some friends in the Blaue Salon.' 'Actually, I am supposed to stop by Ambassadeurs at midnight,' Gert says. In my ignorance, I am informed that this is the newest extension of the Barberina. Gert and Maria then discuss the quality of the various jazz bands and tango groups in the big hotels, in the Palais am Zoo, in the Valencia, etc. I somewhat timidly introduce my experiences from the little Silhouette. 'Why don't we just go across the way here to Eldorado?' Maria says. 'That's where the real bedlam's at. You want chaos, smoking and sport jackets, transvestites, little girls, and great ladies, don't you? Of course, *you're* more for what's proper, Gert — you want elegant dancing and limits, you want to go to Königin.' But, in the end, we decide on something completely different.

A single light shines on the darker stretch of Lutherstraße. A few private cars are parked before the door. The narrow hallway to the lobby is already overcrowded. A friendly manager welcomes us, and at the door to the next room, the master of the house shakes our hands.[1] It's worthwhile to gain his personal protection for oneself, for, as I'm told, far from everyone is welcome here. That is to say, a man may come in and eat and drink, but if his nose displeases the owner of this strange inn, the owner doesn't allow the waiter to accept any payment, but rather will approach the stranger's table himself, and request that he consider this evening a treat on the house — and shouldn't come again. Thus, it's a select clientele here. Heads of industry and culture! And shoulders! And eyebrows. There in the corner sit both the agreeably voluptuous woman and the faintly smiling one who sang about best friends at the revue.[2] And near the piano — impressive even as a silent observer — is the red-haired

---

1   Hessel is describing Rudolf Schlichter's restaurant.
2   Margo Lion and Marlene Dietrich.

mistress of the grotesque. She bursts out laughing. Across from her, the fat colossus from the North Sea coast, who pours out German poetry by day and foreign drinks at night, bellows his well-known cry, with which he rings in the second, merrier half of his evening. But the neighbours give a gentle *shh!* — for standing on the piano, her head ducked near the ceiling, a petite woman in a sailor blouse gestures as she prepares for the song about the maidens of Camaret. She sings in French like her countrywoman, her idol in Montparnasse. And anyone who's spent enough time in Paris understands the song's dangerous words, which now rise into a sort of ecclesiastical melody. The others smile along, clueless and thankful. We listen as we stand in the throng, then we take seats in a corner, at the bar. I look about while Gert and Maria dance. Almost all of the few people of my acquaintance who possess a love of art and lust for life are here.

Gently booming, a stentorian voice calls me by my first name.[3] It belongs to the man who once turned a little corner restaurant in Paris into the 'Dôme', and who is now a famous painter here. In fact, I also know the beautiful Russian edging in next to him. He generously grants her his presence, and critically, through his eyeglasses, he observes a pair of youths, literature's latest, seated reverently across from him. Nearby, the slow, sympathetic smile of the abbot-faced man, who captured the better part of German and foreign literature in his *Bestiarium*,[4] is addressed toward the poet's two grown daughters

---

3 The stentorian voice belongs to Walter Bondy.
4 Franz Blei's 1920 *Das große Bestiarium der deutschen Literatur* satirised prominent German writers.

whom he watched play as children, and who've become world-travellers and conquerers in the meantime.

A new batch of arrivals forces their way through the narrow corridor of dancers. But we're staying. The young bartender is too good a host. We stay until — suddenly — it's three o'clock and some of the chairs are already standing upside-down on the tables. Maria still wants to take us to the ladies' club around the corner, but I'm out of luck there. Even today, when we belong to a member's retinue, its gates remain closed to us. But Gert gets us into Künstler-Eck, where we spoon up a splendid chicken soup under gothic vaults. And now we can move on into the dawning day. Schwannecke still has a side entrance open for their gang. And what's more, Gert knows an association for restaurant employees that opens its doors in the middle of the night and serves food and drink until noon. He's a member there too. We could sit there between the night's last departures and the day's first arrivals, between singers and waiters, actresses and charwomen. But that's enough for today. Knowing that you could keep going for a long time lulls a body so pleasantly.

I've often noticed certain newspaper advertisements and placards carried by publicity men: 'Little Walter the soul-soother with the golden heart, Berlin's best-known life of the party ... Meeting point for broken hearts, once again daily ... Widows' ball for older youths in the magnificent Reception Hall Ackerstraße ... Traditional German ball, older youths only, lively ball music ... Little Claire's stately widows' ball is the talk of the town. The elite only meet on Auguststraße.'

Sometimes, it's condensed to: 'Elite widows' ball', where 'elite' may refer to the widows or to the ball. The one on Elsässer Straße reads, 'High-class ladies, no admission for gentlemen under 25'. Indeed, there isn't. At the entrance of such a dance palace, I've observed how one boy wanted to show his papers as evidence of his maturity, but the man at the till rejected him contemptuously, saying, 'We can see for ourselves!', and didn't let him in.

Since I was visibly old enough, I recently ventured to attend such a ball for older youths; I think it was in the Kaiser Friedrichstraße in Charlottenburg. With a polite 'Surely, I shan't disturb,' the director of the event sat down with us. He wore a frock coat, similar to the one that our professor wore threadbare during winter semester of the tenth grade. The club, he said, was still new, just about to establish its regulations. This building, as it were, once belonged to a Freemason lodge, which Kaiser Friedrich himself had dedicated. We could still see the rings painted on the walls from the lodge days. Back then, this was a ceremonial hall. (It's true, there were really such rings, under dedications of the sort that you read on beer mats.) And below, where the Evangelical Society is now housed, once stood the coffin for the oath.

The director jumped up, together with a distinguished lady with heavy embroidery on her silk dress and somewhat unevenly fat legs, and led a polka-mazurka. Several couples could perform this historical dance without needing to look at the movements of the couple dancing before them. After that, the founder of the club came to us again and informed us that he was employed by day as a craftsman (as he put it), and that by founding the club he intended to promote cordial and neighbourly camaraderie among men. Disruptive elements who, for example, might overstep their bounds with a lady would be eliminated. (We were too unfamiliar here to risk anything of the sort.)

In the meantime, the man who had actually been hired to lead the dancing commenced the so-called 'Ice Skate Dance'. He was gaunt, wearing a swallow-tail coat. At certain turns in this dance, his partner clapped her hands once, sharply, and the others imitated her. But the leader of the dance just made an elegant flourish with his right hand. Some couples had an exceedingly dainty manner of holding each other, with splayed fingers and high elbows. Some gentlemen placed a handkerchief between their hand and the lady's back. I observed that the more advanced the gentleman's youth was, the lower his hands drifted down the lady. Were these 'elements'? Ladies who danced together did not exhibit the intimacy we know from certain other venues, but rather ironised the odd coupling with glances and gestures. It was often ladies' choice, when ladies who happened to be free could 'cut in' — as the experts put it — and take away any other lady's partner. It resulted in some pretty and courteous moments.

Once you've become a member, the club director informed us, the wardrobe also becomes cheaper. Then he rose again to give a brief oration, in which he stressed the merits of the traditional German dances, and called on the ladies and gentlemen present to display friendliness. The band offered up a *prosit* to this cordiality as they received fresh beer.

After this experience, I felt I understood the balls for older youths, which nonetheless seem to play a certain role in Berlin life. You're sure to find friends there. Socially, perhaps, they have a similar effect to the matchmaking institutes whose announcements one reads in the newspapers and on notices pasted to buildings. Now when I read: 'Round dances except Mondays, Thursdays, and Fridays reverse ball', I know what it means.

The balls at which connections are made via so-called table telephones aspire to fewer socio-moral designs. They occasionally have hanging fountains, and they always have what their advertisements describe as 'terrifically merry masses of visitors'. They promise something 'magnificent', 'artistic', 'intimate'. They take place in the 'most cultivated luxury locations in the world', on glass flooring, near the 'high-life bars' and 'exquisite restaurants'. In the most famous of these brightly lit ballrooms, there is a wonderful combination of water and light in revolving, colour-changing basins. According to the brochure, these marvels not only please the eye and elevate the mood, they also provide for the circulation of fresh air. The invention of the table telephone is very psychological: you see, the average Berliner is hardly as self-confident as he would like to seem. But on the telephone, he screws up his courage. (The telephone is very befitting of him, after all. Instead of 'farewell', nowadays he's accustomed to saying 'Well, then ring me up sometime', or 'I'll call you in the next few days'.) And he's reassured by the management's appeal written in verse, which he finds in the interesting brochure:

Don't be bashful, ring her up,
You'll see if she likes you soon enough.

Yes, the ballroom is, as Germany's most popular new verb expresses, completely 'focused' on its guests.

In the half-light of tinted lamps hanging in a number of smaller halls and rooms in the north as well as the west, same-sex couples circulate, here the girls and there the lads. Sometimes the girls are dressed, in a more or less pleasant manner, as men, and the lads as ladies. Over time their appetites, once a bold protest against the dominant moral laws, have become a rather harmless pleasure, and visitors who like to dance with the opposite sex are also allowed into these mellow orgies. They find a particularly favourable environment here. The men learn new nuances in tenderness from the female cavaliers, their partners learn from the masculine ladies, and your own 'straight'-ness becomes a peculiar stroke of luck, as it makes you seem rather exotic. Oh, and the light fixtures are positively magnificent: wooden or metal lanterns with serrated frames, reminiscent of the fretwork of our boyhood.

Before, it seems to me, everything must have been more sinful. Apparently, matters of desire were more calibrated to their level of danger back then. Today, Reinhardt's chamber plays offer distinguished artistry in the place where a steaming violet and golden dance hall once stood.[5] There, before our shocked young eyes, tall corseted figures twirled in threadbare

---

5   Max Reinhardt (1873–1943) organised his *Kammerspiele* in a building next to
    Deutsches Theater.

ball gowns with breasts that were sometimes bare to the nipples, veiled and accentuated by tulle. Crackling petticoats tormented our senses, and when, to a somewhat clumsy can-can, skirts were gathered and shrill voices sang the hit tune about the peach on the tree, we became ill at ease. Wiser fellows found something for the heart in the ballrooms of the outlying districts, in Südende and Halensee, where good girls with principles and careers outnumbered the so-called 'rejects'. They had hands washed to redness, and peculiar violet perfumes that were in constant conflict with nature.

Those were the days when the Palais de Danse bloomed for the extravagant among us. There, the ladies were Babylon and Renaissance, with certain pre-Raphaelite embellishments and variations. In those bygone days, they arrived in droshkies or automobiles from the Bavarian Quarter, pressed the money for the coachman or chauffeur discerningly into the porter's hand, and took a seat on the stools at the bar. Some of them pursued careers. Bakers' daughters became duchesses. One is supposed to have even made it to royal heights, though in society she didn't achieve the same degree of *'reçue'* as the new countesses and duchesses. Now, you wouldn't recognise this Palais today. What did I see when I recently made the mistake of stumbling in? Some lively, lusty people from Meseritz or Merseburg had 'gone out' with Berlin relatives they were visiting, expecting to see half the world, but only a declining, timid quarter turned up ...

A Tour

Enormous cars are parked on either side of Unter den Linden near Friedrichstraße. Liveried men with gold letters on their caps stand before them, inviting passers-by on a tour; over there, one of the firms is called 'Elite'; over here, 'Cheese'. Do I want a life of ease, or guileless petty bourgeois existence? — I'll take 'Cheese'.

So now I'm seated on a leather seat, surrounded by real foreigners. They all seem sure that they'll finish the tour between eleven and one; the family of hyphenated Americans to my right even speaks of continuing on to Dresden in the evening. In multiple languages, the driver asks the guests he's just lured in if they understand German and if they are hard of hearing; it's nothing to be ashamed of, it just affects where you're seated. You get more air up front, but in back you can hear better.

Red writing in English on the white flag in front of me: 'Sightseeing'. What insistent redundancy! All at once, the entire right half of our travel group rises, while I and the others on the left are commanded to remain seated and present our faces to the photographer, who is lifting the cap from his lens there on the side-walk, turning me into a permanent piece of tourism in his group photo. From out of the depths, a native hand reaches up with picture postcards. We lord over it all, we tourists, we foreigners! The lad in front of me, who looks like a dentist, purchases an entire album, first for the memories, then later probably for his waiting room. He compares Old Fritz[1] on glossy paper with the real bronze statue, which we're slowly driving past — he's sitting up very high on his steed in an unforgettable posture, arms akimbo under his broad coat, with a walking stick, and his famed tricorner slanting a bit across his head. He looks over our heads at the pilasters and windows of the university, which was once his brother's castle. He doesn't look benevolent, at least as far as we can tell from below. We're nearly eye-to-eye with the crowd of peers and heroes that decorate his pedestal. Things are a bit tight for them between the wall and the stone precipice. They're held together by four horsemen at the corners of the pedestal, who aren't letting anyone off.

Now we're gliding past the long facade of the library, its sunny side. Silks, leathers, and metals entice from the marquees of elegant shops. The lace curtains at Restaurant Hiller awaken distant memories of happy hours, the nearly forgotten fragrance of lobster and Chablis, the old porter who led you so discreetly to the *cabinets particuliers*. I tear myself away — I'm a foreigner here, after all — only to be caught up again. Travel agencies, mesmerising displays of world maps and globes, the magic of the little green books with red notes,[2] seductive names of distant cities. Ah, those blessed departures from Berlin! How

---

1 For a time, Berliners called the equestrian statue of Friedrich the Great on Unter den Linden by his nickname *Alte Fritz*, 'Old Fritz'.

2 Griebens travel guides were popular in Germany between the wars (during which time Michelin did not update its famous red guides for Germany).

callously one leaves our beloved city.

But pay attention now. We're turning onto Wilhelmstraße. Our driver announces in strange American-sounding German: 'We are now approaching the street that houses the government of Germany.' It's quiet here, almost like a private driveway. Two large-paned lanterns extend an old-fashioned invitation in front of the pastel-yellow facade, behind which Germany's foreign policy is decided. What mellow oil-light might have burned within them, back when they were new? But our driver doesn't allow us to sink into this peace; he draws our gaze to the enormous building complex across the way and cries, himself impressed: 'All that's the judiciary!' — 'And here,' he continues, 'filled with gold from cellar to ceiling, the Ministry of Finance.' That's a joke that only the real foreigners can laugh about.[3] But I comfort myself with the lovely expanses of Wilhelmplatz, the flags fluttering on the Hotel Kaiserhof, the green flourishes growing about the rafters of the pergola at the entrance to the subway, and with General Zieten's hunched Hussar back.[4]

A chaos of towers, bulges, parapets, and wires: 'Leipziger Straße, the most important shopping street in the metropolis!' But for the time being, we're only crossing it. We drive farther down Wilhelmstraße, past many antique stores. (A memory surfaces of the criminally beautiful days of inflation. Wendelin,

---

3   During the period in which this book was written, the Weimar Republic struggled with war reparations, racing inflation, and the global economic depression.

4   Wilhelmplatz was renamed Thälmannplatz by the GDR, and in the 1980s was covered with apartment complexes. Before its destruction, it featured a number of bronze sculptures of Prussian generals, Hans Joachim von Zieten among them.

do you still remember Mr. Krotoschiner back then in his store, staring at the chair with the crest between the Pomeranian cupboard and the Trentino table!)[5] We pass a building by a well-known architect. Older memories of ambitious youth arise, when all one needed to do was study. It was here I heard many instructive lectures.

At Prince Heinrich's palace, we stop for a moment to look through the beautiful hall of columns into the old courtyard and its windows, as well as at the simple building adjoined to it. Both have the light-brownish colour that the poet Laforgue noticed in many Berlin palaces when he came to Berlin in the 1880s to read to the Kaiserin. He called it *couleur café au lait* and it seemed to him to be the predominant colour of the capital. In the world of Wilhelmstraße and many other parts of the city, that is still true today.

Our hasty driver doesn't stop at the well-known museums on Prinz Albrechtstraße. Most of the passengers look over at the big garden behind the state parliament building. I look into the windows of the National Library of Art, where collections await tranquil visitors, with beautiful images of masquerade costumes from the magnificent Lipperheide Collection. What I'd really like to do is get out of the car and go see my dear pictures, but today my duties are that of a foreigner, and I shouldn't linger too long on the site of the old Museum of the Decorative Arts, which itself has been uprooted so often.[6]

---

5 Hessel is mischievously inserting a scene from his 1927 novel *Heimliches Berlin*.
6 The Museum of Decorative Arts was founded in 1868, relocated in 1881 and again in 1921.

Most of its collection is now in the castle. The students of the decorative arts once threw the best *Karneval* celebrations in Berlin, but those now take place in Charlottenburg since the art schools have been relocated there. As a true *laudator temporis acti* (one who praises times gone by), of course I shan't believe that they're as good there as they were here. Oh, even the little parties that were thrown on the top floor here after the art school moved were unforgettable. We glide past the bulging High Renaissance structure of the Ethnological Museum. It too is only named; nothing is said of Turfan or Gandhara, Inca or Maori. Our leader is more interested in announcing, far in advance: 'Vaterland, Café Vaterland, the biggest café in the capital city!' The foreigners stare at the building's gaudy cupola, and those who have already experienced some Berlin evenings advise the others to visit this monster establishment with its many departments, this culinary ethnological museum by Kempinski, with its panoramas lit up at night.[7]

Yes, they should visit. What good do our old palaces and museums do them? What they want is colossal Germany. So, just venture there this very evening, my good people, in the old Piccadilly, now known as Haus Vaterland! You'll find food from the fatherland and abroad. Once the elevator has carried you up from the opulent foyer, you can drink a traditional vintage and gaze into the panorama, while a thunderstorm is enacted for you over hilly vineyards, rivers, and ruins. Once the sky clears,

---

7   Haus Vaterland featured various ethnically themed restaurants, with panoramic scenery and lighting displays. It was opened by the Kempinski family of restaurateurs in 1928. It had previously operated under various concepts and names, including Picadillyhaus.

Rhenish girls will do a jig for you under clusters of grapes to a tune played by students in velvet jackets. You must see it. From there, please stroll into the bodega, where menfolk with brightly coloured cloth wrapped about their heads and torsos will bring you something fiery to transport you to a Spanish *taberna*. The two bashful Spanish ladies from Ackerstraße, sitting in the corner there, will have their spirits raised by a dance performance. When you enter the Wild West bar, according to the program, you'll experience all of the romance of the American prairie. Buy the program, by all means! Then you'll know right away how you're supposed to feel. What is charming Vienna like at the Grinzing Heuriger restaurant? Dusk falls before the visitor's eyes. What does Hungarian wine on a sun-smouldering Hungarian grassland make your heart ache for? To linger, that's what. What awaits us in a Turkish cafe? Fairytale magic from the *Thousand and One Nights*. Don't miss out on sitting on a taboret at tables with genuine Arabic writing on them, drinking the strongest Berlin-Turkish *mokka double* anywhere. You can see your neighbour with his cigar stub mirrored in the glass wall that separates the guests from the Bosporus panorama, as if he were sitting in the foreground of the picture, at a table with a hookah.

But now you're thirsty for a beer, and you'll find it at the Munich Löwenbräu, which according to the program, is decorated with *joie de vivre*. The girls waiting on you speak with a more Bavarian accent than the Bavarians do, just for your benefit, and they wear straw hats with feathers, blue jackets, and ruffled striped skirts. Sometimes they yodel along if it suits the music, which is played by the Buam brothers, who are wearing suspenders. Their pants are patterned with a decorative Bavarian design. There is also an artistically executed glass window here with a view of the 'romantic wilderness scenery around the Eibsee'. And the show is already getting started. The hall darkens. Lights go on in the Eibsee Hotel. Sparing no costs, the management provides *alpenglow*. As soon as the hall brightens, a trio takes the stage: lad, lass, and fool, as if they'd come straight from the now-defunct Oktoberfest exhibition on Kaiserdamm. The two competing suitors hit each other over the head with real barrels. No, the management doesn't spare any costs. If you still want to go into the big ballroom, which 'is a deserving equal to the glamour of the most beautiful ballrooms in the world', and you want 'the opportunity to dance on incandesent parquet', you'll have to pay three marks extra, but they'll be taken off your food and drinks total. In exchange, you'll see a ceiling of polished polychromatic mirrors, upheld by palm trunks as columns. 'Deutsche girls' in veils of gauze brush against you on their way up to the stage. A muscular, bathing-suited young man dances for you with a lady who, apart from a pair of bathing trunks, is only wearing something like a brassiere; he dances with her, spins her as she hangs with just her wrists looped around his neck, performs manoeuvres with her. Then the German girls slip down to perform a sort of synchronised swim routine on the floor and sing about our age, the age of sports.

Now you are granted relief from so much performance. A larger-than-life teddy bear sits by the window, which the girls hug as they brush by, and you walk past it out onto the open balcony. In the bright night you see old Berlin's yellow-brown Potsdam train station, the same sober one that our guide is pointing to now in the daylight.

Excursioners in light-coloured skirts and shift dresses climb the steps leading up to the station. Those lucky things, enjoying such a nice autumn day. Some also go through the narrow entrance to the little Wannsee train station. What I'd really like to do is follow them. A sailboat, or even just a paddleboat.[8] Potsdam and the Havelsee, the secret soul of Berlin, otherworldly places here on earth! And today a weekday. But now we're arriving at Potsdamer Platz. The first thing to say about it is that it isn't really a plaza at all, but rather what they call a *carrefour* in Paris, a crossroads, an intersection; we don't really have the right word for it in German. That Berlin once came to an end at the city gate here, with country roads branching off from it — you'd have to have a well-informed eye to recognise that from the shape of the intersection. The traffic here is so heavy in such a tight space that I'm often impressed at how smoothly it flows. The many flower baskets and flower saleswomen are soothing. And in the middle stands the famed traffic-light tower, watching over the action in the streets like a referee's chair in tennis. The huge advertisements on the buildings' walls and roofs look strangely sleepy and hollow in broad daylight. They're waiting for nighttime to awaken. Sharp and smooth, the glass form of the renovated Telschow confectionary building represents the

---

8   Wannsee and Havelsee are lakes that were day-trip destinations that could be reached by train.

newest Berlin. The corner with Cafe Josty remains in the old days. But on the other side of Bellevuestraße — once concealed behind a high wall covered in posters — there's something completely new, a department store with a Parisian name. Will it be as beautiful as the Wertheim department store, Messel's masterpiece behind the foliage on Leipziger Platz? We're allowed to cast a quick glance down Bellevuestraße, which is increasingly becoming a Berlin Rue la Boétie. Art gallery sidles up to art gallery. And the window displays in the fashion boutiques become ever more exquisite, more like still-lifes. Even the private cars, big and small, waiting in the bay of the driveway in front of Hotel Esplanade seem to have benefitted from modernity. Their bodies are ever-improving combinations of hull and cap, with wonderful colours.

A green light in the traffic tower. We circle Potsdamer Platz and drive along the white columns of the two little gateway temples. According to colloquial Berlin humour, the bronze General Brandenburg is talking to his counterpart General Wrangel about the weather. ('Rotten weather we got t'day,' says Wrangel, extending a hand, holding his ceremonial field-marshal's baton, in front of him. 'Utter shit,' replies Brandenburg, keeping his right hand flat.) More ladies selling flowers stand in long rows to the left and right of these warriors. The side entrance to the Wertheim department store stands before us with narrow, proud buttresses and metal ornamentation. The gaze wanders from the shining new materials in its tall display windows to the bowls, plates, and cups made of white or subtly coloured old-Berlin porcelain there in the building that houses the national — once royal — factory.

The lordly manor nearby seems empty, as if it were for rent; supposedly they've got the State Council and the Social Welfare offices quartered there for want of lords at the moment.

The Ministry of War next door also seems rather outmoded. Even most Reichswehr proceedings are handled elsewhere. A couple of tiny stone soldiers in old-fashioned uniforms stand over the entryway like the toys of bygone royal children, in whose palaces and gardens toy cannons were to be seen. A few giants or Atlases carry a huge stone globe above the Ministry of the Postal Service, which our guide points out to us on the next corner. Hopefully, they won't disrupt traffic by dropping it in the street. Such globes are to be found at several locations in Berlin; they are among the horrors of the last years of the previous century, which now are being cleared away from various privately owned buildings, in massive clean-up efforts. I personally know of one on a major commercial street in Schöneberg, and a no less imposing one of glass stands in the Bavarian Quarter. Since it's not even supported by a reliable colossus like the one here over the postal ministry, I'm always afraid that it will come rolling down, and I hope that it will be eliminated with the next major renovation. It could be put to use in a museum for neo-Wilhelmine architecture and sculpture; this could ultimately be a repository for much of the irritating public and private ostentatiousness lying around the city. The best thing about this massive corner building is that it houses a collection of old vehicles; there are postal coaches and early locomotives in miniature, and above all, a lot of old stamps and

seals, a feast for the memory of anyone who 'traded' Thurn-
and-Taxis[9] and Old Prussia for Guatemalan hummingbirds and
the swan of Australia.

Mauerstraße curves off to the left and around the corner
to the right, a pleasant break from this world of right angles. It
traces the path of the old city wall, and it is said that the soldier-
king Friedrich Wilhelm I, who blanketed all of Friedrichstadt
with lovely buildings in rank and file, was vexed by the inevitable
curvature of the old street. Before we've gotten a closer look
at either of the (also round) domed churches — Bethlehem
Church to the right, and Schleiermacher's domain, the Holy
Trinity Church,[10] to the left — our driver is already moving on.
And instead of gazing at old church walls, we're looking at the
fur, linen, silk, and steel of extravagant window displays. Before
the massive naked stone girls over the entryway can lure us into
the Tietz department store, we turn toward Gendarmenmarkt.
Even from afar, the two patina-ed church domes and the green
winged horse on the roof of the theatre gleam against the dust-
blue sky. Now we stop. I stare at the 'stage entrance'. You others,
you real foreigners, have never stood waiting here, as students,
to see the sublime actress from the *Maid of Orleans* emerge. You
are shown the two churches with the famed domed towers by
Gontard, which Friedrich the Great had him add there,[11] and it

---

9 'Thurn-und-Taxis', a German noble family who operated postal services in
   Europe between the 16th and 18th centuries.

10 Friedrich Schleiermacher (1768–1834), theologist and philosopher, preached in
   the Holy Trinity Church from 1809 to 1834.

11 Carl von Gontard (1731–1791) was a German architect. Though he did not
   create either church on Gendarmenmarkt, he designed the towers added to
   both in 1785.

is emphasised that the one is a German and the other a French cathedral. Both church towers are significantly more grandiose than the older churches huddled shyly next to them. Happily, the theatre is a wonderful unity. Schinkel erected it on the remaining walls of the national theatre, from the Iffland-era,[12] that was destroyed in a great fire. Oh, the beautiful stairway up to its proud front hall with the slender Ionian columns! Though you've never climbed it. Access for your basic visitor was there under the stairs. Ultimately, the stairway was reserved for the royal court, back when this was still a royal theatre. Begas's statue of Schiller stands somewhat haplessly before the whole thing. He would have preferred to be a plain old mossy Triton fountain. Instead, he stands there performing his social duties in a toga, with several pretentious ladies on his pedestal, representing poetry, drama, history, and philosophy.

The foreigners are made aware of the State Bank of Prussia, formerly the 'Royal Prussian Maritime Trading Company', while I peer over at the famed wine tavern where Ludwig Devrient[13] liked to tipple with E.T.A. Hoffmann, who lived on this square at a time when the Gendarmenmarkt was surrounded by palatial state-owned buildings. You must think of Hoffmann's 'My Cousin's Corner Window' and how, in his Warsaw dressing gown with his big pipe in hand, he looked out

---

12 August Wilhelm Iffland (1759–1814), actor and playwright, was director of the national theatre from 1796 until his death.

13 Ludwig Devrient (1784–1832), German actor. There is a famed watercolour of Devrient and Hoffmann drinking together at the sekt bar Lutter & Wegner, the establishment Hessel is hinting at.

over the lively Berlin marketplace.[14]

We go around a corner and now we're on one of these strange oblique-angled plazas. A horrid building used to stand nearby where political prisoners were interned. Now an industrious business quarter has sprung up all around. The only old-time things left are the plots of land; this is where the various incarnations of Wallstraße begin, as well as the terrain of the old Friedrichswerder quarter. This is the third Berlin, outside both of the old cities that combined to form it: the old Berlin on the far side of the river and the nearer old city of Cölln on the Spree. Here we take a right, past the angels praying before the transom windows of the hospital run by the grey sisters of holy Elisabeth.[15] Farther along Alte Leipziger Straße, we pass the wonderful corner at Raule's Hof.[16] Our leader turns onto the broad avenue leading north, past the reddish brickwork of the Reichsbank, designed by Hitzig. He also built the stock exchange, which spurred a veritable renaissance in business and industry for a Berlin whose wealth was accumulating in the eighteen sixties and seventies. Both buildings shook off the modest classicism of the Schinkel school, and were in any case better than that which came afterwards, though they did clear the way for the Wilhelmines to dabble in the old styles.

---

14 Ernst Theodor Amadeus (E.T.A.) Hoffmann (1777–1826) was a Prussian Romantic author, a jurist, composer, music critic, draftsman, and caricaturist. His short story 'My Cousin's Corner Window' is essentially an extended description of the marketplace.

15 The Elisabeth Hospital, today known as the Evangelische Elisabeth Klinik.

16 Benjamin Raule (1634–1707), entrepreneur, erected a residential building on Alte Leipziger Straße and created a narrow lane connecting it to Adlerstraße. Both the building and lane bore his name. Neither exist today.

Our next destination, the Friedrichswerder Church on Werderscher Markt in Schinkel's so-called 'modified gothic' style remains absolutely innocent. It is an upright old Prussian construction, in the brown brick that we know from a host of other churches and train stations in our good city, which looks more dutiful than devout, commemorating 'loyalty and frankness'[17] more than mysticism. Above the entryway, a stern iron angel slays a trespassing dragon, not gazing dreamily into the distance — unlike his older kin of wood, stone, or paint — but staring directly at his victim. Do the elegant saleswomen and clients of the large fashion house across the street ever look up at him? Do they sympathise with the fact that he's so occupied with his mission, or would they rather he dreamed a bit into the unknown, and beyond?

Across the way is the Schleusen Bridge over the Spree and the Schloßplatz, the palace square. For those who are craning their necks to observe the construction, our guide promises that afterwards we'll come back, but first we want to take a little tour through old Berlin. Then suddenly we have to skip that because there's so much else we have to do. But take my advice, foreigners and fellow tourers: if you're in the area again and have the time, get a little lost here. Here, where there are still real lanes, little buildings huddle up against one another, thrusting forth their gables, completely unknown except to a few connoisseurs, neither as empty nor as far away as the really notable buildings are. No, they are densely populated by

---

17 From the 18th-century folk song 'Üb immer Treu und Redlichkeit' ('Always Be Loyal and Frank').

naive people who descend steep staircases with broad wooden landings, or look out of beautifully framed windows, over flower baskets and birdcages.

Peter is the patron saint of fishermen, and the church we're driving around is named after him. It is the sanctum of the fishermen of old-Cölln. Another holy entity enshrined in the hearts of the Cöllners and Berliners is there on the bridge. It's Saint Gertrude, the abbess who founded hospitals and hospices for travellers. Spittelmarkt takes its name from the Hospital of St. Gertrude, a remnant of which stood in the form of the little St Gertrude's Church in the middle of the idyllic marketplace until the 1880s. It has become one of the busiest squares, surrounded by the tallest commercial headquarters in the city. A student kneels before the saint on the bridge, and is offered a libation. Doesn't she see that he's leading a stolen goose on a line, or could it be that she mercifully overlooks it? A friend to the wanderer, she is also dear to the souls of the dead on their journey. According to a folk legend, they turn into mice and come to St. Gertrude in the night following their death, to St. Michael the night after, and on the third night to their eternal hereafter. That's why there's a herd of mice on her pedestal. St. Gertrude holds a distaff. She is a relation of Mother Hulda and the pagan goddess from which Mother Hulda developed,[18] and she watches over the flax harvest and the spinner women. But the spring flowers at her feet represent the gratitude of

---

18 A figure from *Grimm's Fairy Tales* who was probably originally derived from the Germanic goddess Frigg, Mother Hulda (also Frau Holle) is a sage-type character who rewards a hardworking stepdaughter in a story similar to *Cinderella*.

the country folk, whose fields and meadows the Mistress of the Mice protects from the animals under her spell. The statue described here so extensively is no great masterpiece, but so much happens around it that I can report on it as Pausanias did on the sacred masonry of Greece.

Gertraudenstraße leads us to the Cölln fish market, which was once Cölln's main square along the Spree. Until thirty years ago, the Cölln city hall stood here. But a more peculiar building from olden times disappeared nearly a hundred years ago. I'm referring to the madhouse, where they used to put drunks in the old days, so that they could sleep off their inebriation. Though the madhouse is no longer standing, not far from here is another ancient building where things can get really mad. It's at the end of Fischerstraße, which leads from the fish market past old lanes to Friedrichsgracht — the Nußbaum Inn. They claim that it's Berlin's oldest building, and that *Landsknechte*[19] swilled there with the wenches of Berlin-Cölln. It has a high medieval gable. If you really want to understand it, you have to go there late at night, when a peculiar group of guests has gathered. You'll see silk blouses and aprons next to each other at the same table, fishermen's and wagoner's smocks alongside frock coats. Under the innkeeping certificates on the wall hang genuine pictures by Zille, given as a gift by the master himself.[20] It was here that I first heard the modified 'Lorelei' song, with proud addendums to each strophe:

---

19 German mercenary soldiers in the fifteenth and sixteenth centuries.
20 Heinrich Zille (1858–1929), an illustrator and photographer most famous for his humorous sketches and caricatures.

She combs it with a comb then soaps herself with foam[21]

It's also where I met Ludeken, who called herself 'a pal of Zille's'. After everything she said, she put a finger mysteriously into her mouth, and when she was in high spirits, she would alternately show off the papers that allowed her to practice her profession[22] and her white underwear. Everyone bought her drinks, but in her corner she still secretly poured together what was left by other guests. She sometimes danced with gentlemen; sometimes she danced alone, which was always an uplifting sight. Only when her 'boss' came by did she cower meekly in her corner. She would have to tend to his horses at the crack of dawn, and that wasn't an easy thing to be sober for.

Our car rolls over Mühlendamm: the bridge that connected Cölln and Berlin when they were separate cities, the bridge that connected and separated them. For, at this very spot, the citizens of the two neighbouring cities often beat each other bloody. Two bronze margraves stand at the edge of the bridge: Albert the Bear and Waldemar. They're not in the way, but they don't really need to be here either. They already have their territory throughout our whole Siegesallee.[23] Judging by the old pictures, this Mühlendamm must have been pretty when it was still surrounded by arching depots and junk shops. And the mills to which its name refers were surely more visually pleasing

---

21 A spoof of Heinrich Heine's poem 'The Lorelei'; Heine does depict the siren combing her hair, but he makes no mention of further personal hygiene.

22 Ludeken was a prostitute.

23 A boulevard through the Tiergarten that once featured around one hundred white marble statues.

than the municipal Dammühlen Building, that fake fortress from the 1890s that now houses a city bank. If the construction of Berlin's network of waterways really is completed, and the Mühlendamm lock is renovated to meet the demands of larger ships, this building, among others, will fall, and our city planners and architects will have lovely tasks on their hands.

We stop at Molkenmarkt. We notice a beautiful house there from the Frederician era, Palais Ephraim. Ephraim was the great king's infamous 'Lender Jew', manufacturer of the Friedrich d'or coin, called 'green jackets'. There's a little rhyme about them:

> Inside it's dull, outside it gleams,
> Outside it's Friedrich, inside Ephraim.[24]

You can't look inside this beautiful building — government offices are located there. Outside, the corner building forms a sublime semicircle, with balconies resting on Tuscan columns, Corinthian pilasters, and dainty cherubs over the grillwork. The oldest settlement on the Berlin side of the Spree was around Molkenmarkt, and it's here that we also find the only completely preserved medieval lane, the oft-described and oft-depicted Krögel, so famous that our car stops at the beginning of the street and the passengers get out to walk along this narrow lane next to the water. Supposedly, there was once a canal or arm of the Spree here that was already filled in in the olden days,

---

24 Veitel Heine Ephraim (1703–1775) was Mint Master to Friedrich the Great. He used dubious methods to finance the Seven Year's War, creating the Friedrich d'or coins by stamping Friedrich's image onto Saxon coins, hence the rhyme.

and which allowed traffic to flow from the market and depots to the river. A gateway led to the lane's inner courtyard. In the middle ages, Berlin's only public baths were here. The bathers were served there by the daughters of the city, of whom it was said they 'sat upon dishonour'. They had a sort of uniform, short coats, and they had to wear their hair shorn. So it was a great insult in 1364 when the 'in the know' secretary of the Archbishop of Magdeburg, a frivolous *bon vivant*, called upon an honourable citizen's daughter to accompany him to Krögel. The citizens' rage was understandable, as they marched to the great house where the bishop's retinue was staying, tore the offender from his banquet, and beat him to death in the market. However, on certain occasions, honourable women also came to Krögel. It was customary for bridal festivities to begin with breakfast and a bath there. Then a vibrant, lively procession went down the old lanes, with musicians and jesters at the fore. Their antics were indiscreet, but the bride had to put up with them.

An old sundial we see on a wall comes from a later time. It told the hour to attendants of foreign royalty, who were quartered here while their lords were guests of the prince. Today, there are workshops and small apartments in the prominent upper stories and behind the little windows of the ground floor. One of the residents of this living artefact from the Middle Ages owns a museum with weapons, engravings, and old household items. In the summer, sometimes, the racket from the nearest beach echoes over. Just past the Waisen Bridge, across from Neukölln am Wasser, a subway tunnel emerges from the water, and gravel from its renovations forms a sort of beach. The young folk made use of it, and Paddensprung Beach was opened. Otherwise though, it's very quiet on the Krögel, and at night, in the dying light, when there is no sound from the workshops, the real 'old Berlin', with its timber framework and gables, can emerge here.

A lane leads around from the lively Molkenmarkt to a quiet square where the city's oldest church stands. It is dedicated to the patron saint of travellers and merchants, Saint Nicolas. The massive foundations of a granite tower are all that's left of its old walls; the rest burned in 1380, in one of the many fires that ravaged Berlin. The later parts, chancel and nave, have been heavily renovated. You have to come here some weekday afternoon when the organist is playing in quiet devotion. In the twilight, you can recognise the outlines of a family vault that was carved by Schlüter's chisel.[25] The longer you look at them, the more pronounced the curves of the vases and the baroque draperies become. The gothic hall has many chapels, large and small, with statues from all of the great artistic periods, and it sanctifies the memories of several men who are famous well beyond the bounds of the city. There are portraits of military men, provosts, scholars, councilmen, and their wives. Many bearded heads in ruffed collars and periwigs, crowned with laurels by allegorical female hands, or with halos of stars by cherubs. The crests on the urns are framed in acanthus. A little cupid cries over an hourglass and a dimming torch. A portrait

---

25 Andreas Schlüter (1659–1714), German sculptor and architect, who created important works in Berlin as court sculptor to Friedrich III.

is ringed by the serpent of eternity under winged skulls, all on a dark background.

Like St Mary's Church and Cloister Church, St Nicolas's Chuch became a protestant church, and like the others it also kept some of its old pomp. It's a shame that their halls no longer smell of incense. It's interesting to think that the indulgence-hawking Tetzel[26] preached here, thronged by *tout*-Berlin of that time, who later threw him out of the city gates along with church dignitaries, tradesmen, and White and Black Monks.[27]

The quiet square surrounding the church — this island of dreaminess in the noise of the big city — was once called Nikolai Graveyard, along with the many tombs in the church and outside along its walls. A few very small old buildings still stand here, and when you go into one of them, you can look down into a tiny courtyard. Steep staircases lead up to the apartments, and some of the buildings don't have their own gable walls, they're just 'stuck' to the next building. One of them claims to be Berlin's smallest house, offering private-lunch specials, though it doesn't have an address and it can only be entered via the building next door. On a walk through the old city you can still find houses like that here and there. Often they're just three windows wide. The double front door opens directly onto the ground-floor apartment on the right, and on the left it connects to the narrow staircase that starts at the doorsill and climbs to the upper floors.

---

26 Johann Tetzel (1465–1519), Dominican friar. Martin Luther drafted his '95 Theses' partly in reaction to Tetzel's selling of indulgences.

27 Cistercian and Benedictine monks, respectively, called so because of the colour of the choir robes worn over their habits.

We drive back to Mühlendamm, then down An der Fischerbrücke Straße, and cross the island bridge to Neukölln am Wasser. Here, and across the way on Friedrichsgracht, there are a few old buildings, some with pointy, pitched roofs, some with lovely mansard roofs from the baroque era with garlands under their windows and pilasters subdividing the house fronts. Our car drives too fast to have a look at all of that; we'll have to postpone it until we can walk down the streets and the lanes near the river. Then you'll see curiosities nestled in among the picturesque, like this gigantic rib bone on one of the corner buildings of the Molkenmarkt, or the relief of a man carrying a door on his back on Wallstraße. He's nicknamed Samson because of the story about the city gate of Gaza. According to folklore, this figure is supposed to remind us of the days when the Köpenick Gate stood here, and in its day, the hasp was stored in this building. But the more entertaining version goes: a poor cobbler eked out a meagre existence here with his wife and many children. When Friedrich the Great and his lottery director Casalbigi — whom we know from Casanova's memoirs — set up a big sweepstakes that earned him a great deal of money and cost his citizens an equally great amount, this cobbler is said to have bought a ticket and glued it to the narrow door out of fear that his children would lose it while playing. It was precisely this poor wretch who had bought the winning ticket. And to prove it, there was nothing left for him to do but to lift the door from its hinges and carry it on his back. And so he trekked, much to the astonishment of his fellow citizens, to the lottery offices. And after he had received his money, he had the image mounted on the wall of the building.

Such tales are plentiful in our storied city. The most famous of them is the oft-told anecdote about the bust of jealousy in Poststraße: the story goes that the soldier-king and upstanding paterfamilias Friedrich Wilhelm I had it mounted on the house of a hard-working goldsmith in order to punish the goldsmith's jealous neighbour.[28]

Now we'll at least want to cast a glance at the bridges while driving by: Waisen Bridge, Insel Bridge, and the beautiful Roßstraßen Bridge, which Chief Municipal Planning Officer Ludwig Hoffmann built, a man to whom Berlin owes much. Nowhere else was and is the Spree so integrated into the city landscape as here. Hoffmann and his staff knew what should be rebuilt in order to match the old, without falling into historicism and dependence like Wilhelm II's 'romantic' planning officer. We come to one of the masterpieces of this artistic scene, Märkisches Museum. The garden around this proud structure is called Köllnischer Park, and you can stroll among chunks of columns and crumbling angels in the greenery, watch children playing, or look at one side of the fortress-museum. All around the thick, angular tower, the various stylistic periods of the area are represented in

---

28 According to legend, Friedrich Wilhelm I was walking down Poststraße late one evening when he saw an industrious goldsmith still hard at work. He rewarded his diligence with commissions from the palace. When the king returned one day, he noticed the wife of a goldsmith across the street making a mocking face at his favoured goldsmith. To punish her, he had a grotesque sculpture of a woman's head mounted on the side of the building with snakes for hair, sticking out a tongue that was also a snake.

brickwork, as they appear in wealthier places: Tangermünde, Brandenburg, etc. And this diversity of forms fits perfectly with the whole building's museum character. Inside is a wealth of knowledge about our city, from the beginning of history here to the days of Theodor Fontane. You can get to know the common people of Hosemann's Berlin,[29] view Berlin interiors from the Biedermeier period, including a parlour of the sort Felix Eberty describes, though in truth you could collect far more Biedermeier items from Berlin's private owners: all of the odds and ends of wallets and silverware, rosewood music boxes, pictures from family registers, autumnal-yellow birchwood furniture, and mahogany cabinets. Yes, I could imagine an entire Museum of Berlin Interiors, where other curiosities from the late nineteenth century could be seen trimmed in plush and hung with tchotchkes, tinted crown-glass windows, plaster angels, and vacation-photo albums. The flora and fauna collection is another extremely exhilarating department of the Märkisches Museum: lovely puzzlegrass and meadow species; reeds, ferns, and grasses; snails and the wonderful ornaments that are wasps' nests.

In front of the museum stands a statue of Roland that is modelled on the Roland of Brandenburg. Cölln's medieval-counterpart city of Berlin lost its Roland very early on. It is said to have stood on or near Molkenmarkt as a symbol of the city's independence. And Friedrich II the Elector robbed the city of her power and forced the bear to subjugate its emblem to his

---

29 Theodor Hosemann (1807–1875), an illustrator and painter who depicted scenes from the lives of Berlin's working classes.

own eagle,[30] removing the statue from the city and hiding it in his fortress. Since no trace of this Roland statue was ever found, the legend arose that the prince had thrown it into the Spree. Since recently, Berlin has a Roland again, on Kemperplatz, which ousted the dreamy green Wrangel fountain of our childhoods, with its friendly sea gods. Now it stands in front of one of the regrettably Romanesque buildings near the Kaiser Wilhelm Memorial Church. But we learn that, due to rampant traffic, it too will soon be cleared away.

We drive back over the Waisen Bridge. To the right, the old Jannowitz Bridge is broken off, a wonderful theatre of ruins and new construction. Between cranes and barges, mountains of rubble and backhoes, the wrecked remains of the old bridge jut out, a Ponte Rotto in the middle of the Spree. They're also working on the city railway arches, whose disrupted brickwork is an incense-scented Temple of Steam, dedicated to that already antique method of 'locomotion'.

Stralauerstraße leads us past the massive city hall that Ludwig Hoffmann built. We look up at its tall tower, two stories of columns capped with a Mediterranean canopy. We turn down Jüdenstraße, and the bronze bears made by Wrba[31] guard the entrance to the city hall's ballroom, valiant totem animals of the people of Berlin. The good old bear of Berlin; he must have become the city's symbol through some slip of

---

30 Roland statues (a statue of a knight bearing a sword) were often placed in medieval northern German cities as symbols of their freedom and rights. The bear is the symbol of Berlin, the eagle of Brandenburg.

31 Georg Wrba (1872–1939), a prolific German sculptor. The bears described in front of the Rotes Rathaus were created in 1906–1907.

folk etymology. Because the word 'Berlin' has nothing to do with bears, the scholars tell us, but rather — here as elsewhere — it is the Wendish word for levee.[32] And just such a levee or dam connected the left and right banks of the Spree in Wendish prehistory, so that even before the days of the Mühlendamm, a union existed between the towns that were later called Berlin and Cölln. But now the bear is our city animal, and the ones by Wrba are particularly charming. The pointy green tower of the Parochial Church is peering down at us. Lovely bell music rings out from it on Sundays and Wednesday afternoons.

There are a couple of ancient buildings on the neighbouring Parochialstraße that will be torn down soon. It's so long overdue that the building inspectors can no longer let people reside there. But often no one really knows who lives in a building, and so posters direct the occupants to vacate the premises. Neighbours call one of them 'the haunted house', because its squatters never show their faces by the light of day. Some of its doors and windows have been removed. Another house is the makeshift site of a strange exhibition. A peace lover has set up his Anti-War Museum there.[33] Outside, he's hung up helmets as flowerpots, the sort they wore in the trenches. Many promising-looking books lie in the window

---

32 'Wendish' is a flexible term for Slavic cultures historically located in what is now Germany. 'Wendish' is sometimes also used to refer specifically to the Sorbian language, but most sources trace the etymology of 'Berlin' to the word for swamp in the now-extinct Polabian language.

33 Ernst Friedrich (1894–1967) was an anarchist pacifist who opened the Anti-War Museum in 1925. It was destroyed by the Nazis in 1933, and he later fled Germany. In 1982, Friedrich's original museum was re-established in Berlin, where it is still in operation.

display. Steps lead down to a cellar-like room, which abuts the crumbling wall of another building to the rear. Death grins from grisly photos of wounded soldiers, weapon parts, munitions, mobilisation orders, and war bonds promising a golden era. Little helmets and sabres for the dear children at Christmas, pillows embroidered with 'For our brave warrior', ID tags, caricatures of the foreign leaders of that great era, soap-ration cards, tickets for firewood, 'German' tea next to tin soldiers and cups inscribed with 'God punish England'. An instructive collection that will hopefully find a worthy home after this place has been torn down.

A few paces down Jüdenstraße, the entrance to Großer Jüdenhof[34] opens between two buildings — as the epithet suggests, there once was a small Jüdenhof not far from here, which has since fallen victim to a street-widening initiative. But the big one is still quite intact, encompassing a dozen buildings around a courtyard-like square. A stairway with iron latticework leads up to the stateliest building, before which stands an old acacia tree. And under this tree in front of 'the house with the staircase', it is said that the Jews, when they were once again driven out, buried their gold — they certainly knew that the nobleman or prince who chased them away wouldn't be able to do without his 'servants of the royal chamber', as they were

---

34 Großer Jüdenhof was a gated residential area founded by Jewish families in the 12th century. The Jews were expelled from Berlin in the 16th century, the old buildings demolished, and new ones constructed, though the name of the square was not changed. The structure of the Jüdenhof remained until it was partially demolished in 1937. The rest was destroyed by bombing in the Second World War.

called, for long.[35] That was back in the times when they resided here behind an iron gate that was locked and guarded at night. They were only allowed to show themselves on the streets wearing their obligatory uniforms: kaftans in certain colours and pointed hats. They weren't allowed to secure a permanent residence, or to do business at markets or trade fairs, and they had to pay large sums of money for protection. Apparently, though, they liked it here: each time they were expelled they came back again as soon as they could, made fortunes, aroused suspicion, and were tortured. The story of a certain Lippold[36] is preserved in detailed description and images: he was held in high regard by the princely court, but was harshly accused by his patron's son and successor, and was sentenced to an agonising death. The executioner, in a light-grey hat with a red band, had to take him from place to place on a special cart for those condemned to death, stopping here and there to subject him to hideous tortures before finally quartering him at the marketplace. The street children ran behind him from corner to corner, having a field day watching the executioner giving the condemned the rod. When more humane days arrived, the Jews moved out of the old ghetto, which has become an utter idyll in the middle of the chaotic city.

Today, there's something similar to a ghetto in another

---

35 *Kammerknechte*, the status of the Jews in medieval Europe, which placed them under a ruler's protection but also gave him the right to tax them.

36 Lippold Ben Chluchim (1530–1573) was a court Jew and mint master under Joachim II Hector, who accumulated large sums of debt during his reign. When the ruler's son, John George of Brandenburg, came to power, he persecuted many people formerly under his father's protection, including particularly harsh treatment of Jews.

location, but only for a short while longer: the Scheunenviertel, which houses a voluntary ghetto in its many little lanes between Alexanderplatz and Bülowplatz, is just about to be wiped from the face of the earth. You'll have to hurry if you want to see the life on its streets, which have strange, militaristic names that don't sound medieval in the least: Dragoon Street, Infantryman Street. The new buildings are already rising, towering over the remains, which are slowly becoming ruins. But for now the men with the old-fashioned beards and sidelocks still walk in slow-moving groups down their streets, speaking Yiddish, while groups of black-haired butchers' daughters are generally lively. Hebraic inscriptions are to be found on the shops and the taverns where people stand up to drink their beer. These streets are still a world of their own, home to the eternal wanderers, who long ago were propelled out of the east in one great wave. Eventually, they will have so acclimated themselves to Berlin that they can be tempted to push farther into the west of the city and to discard the most evident signs of their peculiarity. And it's too bad; the way they live in the Scheunenviertel is nicer than the way they may live later in the clothing factories or the stock exchange.

Our car drives rapidly down Klosterstraße. It doesn't stop before the colonnade of the old Gymnasium zum Grauen Kloster, the oldest secondary school in Berlin. The school grew out of the monastery of the Franciscans, also known as the Grey Friars, and it still houses a formal assembly hall and chapter house within its walls, and a monastery church in its courtyard. It survived a great fire in the year 1380 unscathed, and its walls have preserved more of the Middle Ages than any other church in Berlin. In the dusky chancel, the visitor can admire the monks' fifty pews. They're made of oak and richly decorated with labyrinthine carvings. Symbolic figures are carved into the wall panels above them: strange allegories of the passion story, a money tray with pieces of silver, Judas's betrayal, two faces nestled together that signify his kiss. Torches and lanterns recall the nighttime arrest in the Garden of Gethsemane, chains represent Jesus's shackles, a sword and a clock symbolise Petri's blow at the high priest's servant.

When the Gymnasium was founded, it only took up half of the monastery buildings. The others, up to the storehouse, went to Leonhard Thurneysser, the polymath from Basel. He operated his own book-printing press, type foundry, and workshops for making woodcuts and copper engravings there and in the storehouse. He made gold tinctures and pearl elixirs, essences of amethyst and amber, as well as beauty potions for high-society ladies, each of whom sent him thank-you letters requesting that he not provide the same potion to anyone else. It was said that he had caught Satan in the form of a scorpion in a glass, and that three black monks dined with him daily, who were certainly emissaries from hell.

Past the imposing building that houses the district and local court, we come to the city railway arches and Alexanderplatz, where things currently look disorderly because the whole quarter is being torn up and rebuilt. For this car full of foreigners, there is no time to delve into the secrets of the area surrounding the square. That will have to wait until I take a stroll in the east. We drive a bit down Neue Friedrichstraße, and a bit down Kaiser Wilhelmstraße, until we reach Neuer Markt. Had we been on foot, we would have walked down the narrow Kalandsgasse, recalling the somewhat mysterious Kalands brotherhood which lent it its name, and whose Kalandshof stood in the shadows of St. Mary's church. At first, this old charitable association, whose name still lies in question (the common interpretation that it stems from the word *calendae* is contested), was a brotherhood of 'wretched priests of the priory' who lived according to stringent rules recalling those of the Templars. But it transformed into an obscene group whose lifestyle was so shocking that today, in our country, the term 'Kaland' still evokes a particularly depraved form of idleness.

At Neuer Markt, a large monument to Luther stands in front of St. Mary's church. There, the reformer is outfitted with his obligatory Bible, along with his entire cadre. His comrades-in-arms stand and sit along the broad pedestal of the great stone structure, and two of them are even perched on the sides of the stairs leading up to it.

In the olden days, a gallows stood here for soldiers who had been sentenced to an ignominious death. When it was erected, Peter the Great of Russia was visiting King Friedrich Wilhelm I. The Tzar was very interested in this new execution device, and asked the king to try it out on one of Friedrich Wilhelm's tall soldiers. When the king refused in outrage, Peter said, 'Well, then we can try it with a member of my retinue.' The monarch politely refused this offer. And anyway, it's better that a monument stands there now instead of a gallows. But the very best thing would be nothing at all, or just the colourful market booths of an earlier era. St. Mary's Church is made of broad stone cubes, granite from before the time when they built with brick in Brandenburg.

My dear foreigner, you must see this church from the inside if you have the time. There's a wonderful pulpit designed by Schlüter. And the most stirring things about the pulpit are the two big angels, in throes of ecstasy from their outstretched toes to their upturned necks. Rapture shivers through their downy marble wings. There are beautiful tombs in the chapel: behind the wrought-iron grate, the richly ornamented, sepulchral stone of a patrician couple. Here, like at St. Nicolas's Church and Cloister Church, nobles and patrons were surrounded by the tombs of their ancestors. These churches are a world of their own: the upright gravestones on the walls, the worn sandstone slabs whose coats of arms and helmets become more distinct once you've looked at them for a while, the wooden panels with portraits of the benefactors engulfed by allegory in stone. In addition to all of the tombs in the church and its external walls, you must also imagine the graves of the common folk, which were located on the square in front of the church, where herds grazed and which also served as a space for making rope and bleaching cloth. Increasingly, these graveyards migrated away from the churches. Only a few remain by their house of worship, such as the old parochial cemetery. As early as the reign of Friedrich Wilhelm I, they began to shift the congregations' gravesites out beyond the city gates.

There's one thing left in St. Mary's Church that I need to talk about. In the base of the tower, a twenty-metre long fresco runs the length of the church wall. It was discovered just half a century ago beneath the whitewashing with which it had been concealed in times less sympathetic to images. Clerics and laypeople alternate with Grim Reapers, leading a dance before a blue sky and a green town common. A grimacing monstrosity follows the dance, lurking, making music at the feet of a brown-frocked Franciscan. Next to his pulpit, the roundel (a round dance) of the surplice-clad sacristans begins. A death figure gropes at them, while also reaching his left hand toward the next cleric, connecting the grey Augustinian monk to his mortal neighbour, who, in turn, is linked by death to a church patron in red robes, and so it continues with a Carthusian monk, a doctor — in the Middle Ages, he was counted among the clerics, and here he regards the liquid in a glass with pious dread — the petite canon, the feisty abbot, the flashy bishop, the red hat of the Cardinal, all the way up to the pope's triple tiara. The wall comes to a corner behind the pope, and there the dance is interrupted by an image of He who was crucified. His mother and closest companion raise their praying hands to Him. Then come the worldly: first the emperor with sceptre and crown, clothed in blue-gold and led by Death toward the empress, gathering the train of her dress. The king appears very young in his light-coloured cloth boots. The knight must dance in his armour, the mayor in a fur-trimmed overcoat — and the mayor must put up with the fact that just a Death's-arm's-length away from him, a usurer is dancing the same step: a genteel, fur-trimmed man, no less. A squire in a heavy jacket and bulging stockings, a craftsman in a smock, and a poor blundering farmer follow. The fool in a jingling costume brings up the rear. Many versions of Death — some striding, some creeping, some with one uplifted foot — unite the children of man in the dance. They're not depicted as skeletons, as in most depictions of the Dance of Death, whose bony faces display a rich variety of stiff, derisive grimaces. Here, their gaunt bodies are merely outlined. A white shroud hangs about their shoulders as a cape, leaving their bodies uncovered. And the figure of Death who reaches toward the Holy Father is completely naked.

This is the oldest painting you'll see on any gloomy church walls in Berlin. And beneath it are bitter rhymes in old Low German, partly smudged out, that speak of the inescapable nature of the dance. Though it may not be as famous as the Dance of Death murals in Lübeck, Strasbourg, or Basel, it is grippingly true to life and possesses an authentic Berlin brightness and coolness. The people in the picture actually *did* dance a roundel in celebration of the inevitable loss of life. After one of the great plague years, the joy of existence was particularly strong, as is always the case after that terrible pestilence (and often even as it is raging, to spite it). During this dance, young and old came together in rejoicing and laughter. The cheerful music cut off suddenly with a shrill dissonance, and a quiet, sombre melody rose slowly and transformed into a funeral march. Meanwhile, a young man lay down on the ground and remained there, motionless, like a corpse. The women and girls danced around him, jeering and singing a comic dirge, which was echoed in laughter from all sides. Then, one after another, they approached the corpse and tried to revive him with kisses. After the first part of this grotesque ceremony, all danced a roundel together. During the second part, the men and boys danced around a woman pretending to be a corpse. Then came the kissing, and the rejoicing knew no end.

We cross Spandauerstraße. Before turning south, we catch a glimpse of the Chapel of the Holy Spirit. It was preserved when a new building, the Berlin School of Commerce, was built around it, so that its deeply dipping tiled roof is level with the School's mansard roof. Inside, there's now a lecture hall. Lectures about balance sheets, bookkeeping, and banking echo up to the gothic stellar vault. In the Middle Ages, it belonged to the Pauper's Hospital of the Holy Spirit. Much ivy is twined about the pointed arches of the windows.

We pass the main post office and the city hall, that 'red hall' made of brick and terracotta. A few times on our tour already, we've seen the high tower jutting out over the rooftops, with little columns on its open-work corner ledges, and it will be peering down over us for a while still. Parts of the old town hall, in whose stead this building was erected in the 1860s, were moved to the park of the Babelsberg Palace in Potsdam. The Gerichtslaube, for example, a loggia with allegorical decorations: the ape of lust, the eagle of theft and murder, the boar of debauchery, and a strange bird with a human face and the ears of a donkey, the blood-sucking vampire of avarice and usury.

Alternately heraldic and recapping, the guide shows us the Dammühlen Building, the town hall, and the oldest parts of the palace: the 'green cap' tower and palace apothecary. A couple of street urchins listen in for that one. We poor foreigners seem downright laughable to them. They imitate the guide's explanatory gestures and call out, 'Ya see, that there's water, 'n' in the car's the Zoo-logical Gart'n.'

We suffer in silence until the car drives on, stopping again in front of the Neptune Fountain and the magnificent columns and pilasters on the southern facade of that beautiful building by Schlüter.[37]

Our guide lingers a bit too long by the fountain, which at least has a well-situated water sprite at its edge, with a fishing net in her lap. Beyond her are the former royal stables, about which there is nothing to note except for their imposing dimensions, and which now house a city library with many interesting books about Berlin. During the guide's explanations, my eyes remain on Schlüter's pilasters and window frames, and the statues on the balcony railing. On 19 March, 1848, King Friedrich Wilhelm IV must have appeared on this balcony in order to view the corpses of the citizens that had been brought to the palace from Straße.[38] The crowd of people sang and cried out and all were bareheaded, except for the king, who still had his cap on. Someone cried out 'Hat off!', and he took it off. The bodies were driven through the palace to the cathedral. The procession paused in the castle courtyard, where the king once again had to appear on the gallery, listen to an earful from the crowd, and bare his head.

---

37 Hessel is referring to the Berlin City Palace visited earlier on the tour.

38 This is a reference to the March Revolution, during which Friedrich Wilhelm ceded to public demands for governmental reform, and participated in the public mourning of those killed during the uprisings.

The guide claims that the Eosander Portal and the chapel cupola above it have really only come into their own since the national monument replaced the buildings around the square, which was once called Schloßfreiheit.

Some of us are of another opinion — we long for that modest freedom that can be seen on the old copperplates. It certainly ennobled the palace, just as the cathedrals in old cities were dignified by the market stands and bevy of houses leaning against them, in the days when true splendour dwelled amid true poverty.

Below the portal is the entrance to the palace museum. For the past few years, the decorative arts have been housed on the ground floor and part of the upper floor. And it wasn't so long ago that the palace housed the last members of the family for which it was built. We saw them exiting via the portal and standing on the balcony, where they could speak to the populace. Now all of the rooms in the gigantic construction form a museum. Besides the rooms that have *really* been outfitted as a museum, you can also look at the others whenever you'd like: the king's chambers and staterooms, and even historically preserved living quarters.

Unfortunately, a tour guide is usually around. They don't make it easy to visit palaces. In some of them, such as the delightful garden palace Monbijou, which houses the Hohenzollern Museum, you can wander around undisturbed and observe Old Fritz's walking sticks in peace; his clocks, porcelain, embellished tobacco tins; his mother's rooms, the Chinese cabinet, and the curious wax figures of the princes and princesses. But you rarely have it so good in Berlin, Charlottenburg, or Potsdam. Mostly you're led around, and whatever the guide may say, a better, pithier, and more authoritative version can be found in Baedeker. The worst part is that the pace of the visit depends completely on the guide and his herd. If you aren't lucky enough to get a private tour, you have no choice other than to haphazardly linger in front of a beautiful piece of furniture or painting while the Keeper of the Foreigners rattles off his lines about the whole room. Sometimes you're better off contemplating the amusing presence of this guide — his herd shuffling on felt-slippered feet, appraising notable objects with strange cries and interjections — instead of the relics he oversees.

While we're happy to find that the rooms in the Berlin Palace have been restored to the condition they were in when the emperor lived there, our expert, who knew their former glory, opines that the rooms are now somewhat cold, and describes in detail the Persian carpets that lay here ten years ago, the battle paintings and the portraits. He even shows us the spot where the highly modern electric cigar lighters used to be. In the empress's rooms, while the guide talks about her habits and possessions, the art aficionados among us must look at the marvellous Watteau paintings — if they hope to observe them with any degree of thoroughness — which are interlopers in the rooms of this most un-Watteau-esque of ladies. And when the chaperone in the Charlottenburg Palace winds the atrocious trumpeter clock and lets it blow, claiming that it shocked Napoleon awake when he spent the night here, you hold your ears shut and stare at the charming silks that surrounded sweet cheerful Crown Princess Luise in her slumber, her little stoves, or her striking portrait in a

Prussian cavalry uniform. In rooms like that, you have to linger alone or among kindred souls in order to commune with the spirits that inspired the work of Schlüter and Schinkel and their students and assistants, and to experience the great ages of old Berlin: Prussian baroque and rococo and Prussian classicism.

Some things are revealed to you at first glance: the abundant blooming grandeur of Schlüter's four continents in the great hall; the pure forms and pleasant colours of the Parole Hall, with Schadow's marble grouping of young Crown Princess Luise and her sister; the gold and green of the round domed chamber, which was Friedrich the Great's writing refuge. And you can linger to your heart's content in the inner palace courtyard in front of Schlüter's arched halls. No king bars your entry to the courtyard anymore, and no guide forces you to hurry through.

We stop on the side of the palace with the pleasure garden, in front of its two horsemen, which the Russian emperor gave to the Prussian king in the 1840s. Berlin folk-humour named them 'progress reined' and 'regression spurred'.

The freestanding columns of polished granite at the corners of the terrace also date from this era, golden eagles nesting on top of them. Varnhagen,[39] a modern and critical observer, found these decorations too elegant for the imposing, cumbersome, gloomy building, and the desire to embellish it tasteless. 'The people,' he wrote, 'stand before it and call it unnecessary. They compare it with the epaulettes of the royal footmen, which were too simple for the king — he had crowns added to them.' At that time, just after the revolutionary days of 1848, groups of

---

39 Karl August Varnhagen von Ense (1785–1858), historian of the Romantic era.

workers, students, and teachers still crowded under the lindens and in front of the palace. A court marshal had secured iron bars across the palace gates. The Civil Defence Militia[40] couldn't prevent a large section of these bars being torn down by the workers and thrown into the Spree from the Kurfürsten Bridge. Another, smaller section was carried by the students to the university. Later, people simply accepted things as they were and viewed the bars as a monument to the 18th of March. They turned the palace into a cage, the people said, and made the king pitiable. It was a bit of foolishness on his part to put up the bars after the danger was over. The eagle is still there, though the bars have come down. And viewed from the Lustgarten, the palace is more beautiful, admirable, and historically significant than ever.

Across from the broad palace square, the Lustgarten extends to the steps of the Altes Museum, on a wonderful isle right in the middle of the city. It's not just geographically correct that this district, buffered by water, is called the Museum Island. The world that begins here with Schinkel's hall of Ionian columns is the young Berliner's Platonic Academy — or at least that's what it was for my generation — a hint of what he'll get to see later in the Louvre and the Vatican, in the museums of Florence and Naples and Athens.

But we wanted to stay out in the city and on the street. For a short visit to the museums, Baedeker is excellent; its single and double stars inform us as to what the *consensus gentium* deems

---

40   Civil Defence Militia (Bürgerwehr): 19th-century military units comprised
     citizens forced into service to defend their cities.

exceptionally beautiful and valuable, although this doesn't prevent anyone from making their own discoveries.

From the foyer of the Altes Museum, the visitor passes under the dome of the rotunda, which welcomes you into the heart of things with mostly Roman imitations of Greek statues. It's lovely to be encircled by these marble beings without inspecting them more closely, saving our energy for all of the wonderful things that await us in the archaeological room and the rooms for the fourth and fifth centuries, the Late Period of ancient Egypt, and the Romans. Ancient handiwork in bronze is collected on the top floor, with gold and silver, jewellery, and the grotesque and thrilling terracottas by the masters of Tanagra and their students. In Stüler's Neues Museum, if I might give you some advice, foreigner, don't stay too long in the big stairway with the gigantic frescoes by Kaulbach. They depict the most significant moments of world history, and they would probably serve quite well for primary schools.

In the Egyptian section, you'll find massive statues and sarcophagi, the fair little heads of the queens Tiye and Nefertiti, and, in front of black-and-red-figured vases, you'll sink into that drowsy state in which you're no longer certain: *is it the Seine flowing by outside or the Tiber? Will we be breakfasting in Posillipo or in the Savoy?* Leave yourself plenty of time for the chamber of copper engravings. Don't just look at what's hanging on the walls or lying in the glass cases. They're happy to give you one of the many beautiful portfolios, and you can while away an hour as a scholar of art. It's worth it. And by the time you read these lines, maybe the new museum that Alfred Messel began will finally have been completed. Then you'll see the sublime Altar of Pergamon assembled with its gods and giants.

With regards to the National Gallery, as your guide to Berlin, I must recommend those paintings in which the Berlinesque is immortalised: Menzel's wonderful *Balcony Room* and his *Bedroom*, the courtly *Supper at the Ball*, *Palace Garden of Prince Albricht*, the old *Berlin-Potsdam Railway*; furthermore, the painters of the old city and the life of its people, especially Theodor Hosemann, and Franz Krüger's portraits, and his big paintings of parades. You'll discover the Berlin romantic in landscapes by the great Schinkel, who wasn't really a painter, but rather an architect. He painted them for one of the old patrician houses on Brüderstraße, and if you have the leisure for it, read what Hans Mackowsky wrote about it in his *Buildings and People in Old Berlin*,[41] and keep reading what he wrote regarding this building and others. The bygone city hiding within the current one will materialise right before your eyes. The Kaiser Friedrich Museum would be better named after the man who made it world famous — the Wilhelm von Bode Museum[42] — instead of after that ruler and patron of the arts whose hideous equestrian monument stands before the doors of this chamber of treasures. Regarding this world of paintings and sculptures I have nothing to write here, for although it is Berlin's greatest glory, it nonetheless has nothing to do with our good city itself. You are even farther away from

---

41 *Häuser und Menschen im alten Berlin*. Berlin: Cassirer, 1923.
42 Indeed, since 1956, the Kaiser Friedrich Museum has been known as the Bode Museum.

Berlin here than in other museums' rooms of Greek sculptures, which Prussian classicism at least displayed a longing toward despite themselves — sensibly faded, restrained, opposed to all pomp, and righteously diligent.

But back to the beautiful expanses of the Lustgarten and our touring car. The square is really an island of peace. Viewed from the long palace facade with its broad gates, not a bit of the present day is to be seen — and hopefully won't be for a long time. The only turmoil in this tranquil setting is the cathedral with its many high-renaissance details, niches, halls, and domes. It spreads across a piece of land where a smaller church from Friedrich's days stood until the 1890s. It covers an area of 6,270 square metres, while the Cologne Cathedral only manages to take up 6,160. It is completely unnecessary to enter it, for this massive structure offends every religious and humanistic sentiment with its sheer quantity, materiality, and poorly applied erudition. The acoustics are supposed to be excellent, and to improve them, cords still hang expressly for that purpose from the inner dome of the central building. A marble angel is right to proclaim, 'He is not here, He is risen.' And it's true, He is surely not here. A few lovely tombs are wasted here, associated with the names Peter Vischer and Schlüter. Maybe there will come a day when we impulsively tear down this building and a few others, just as we do now with objectionable private buildings. Then this site will be completely dedicated to the past and to peace.

This place only comes to life anymore when popular assemblies take it over, and it is perfectly suited for that, since the Lustgarten is nothing more than a sand-paved square. Its name recalls an entirely different time, an age when parks were an art, an age of grottoes and grotto-makers. In the days of the Great Elector and his son, a colossal Neptune with grotto and waterfalls were to be seen here, along with fountains, and enormous clams adorning Memhardt's Neue Lusthaus. The 'grotto masters, fountain makers, and stuccoers' had plenty of work there, just as they did later under Friedrich the Great, for whom they built a Neptune grotto in Sanssouci, and a clamshell hall in the New Palace. On Remus Island in Rheinsberg they built the Chinese House. And later the builder of the simple little Paretz Palace erected a colourful clamshell-covered Japanese temple in the corner of a park as a sort of relic from the Rococo era. The final echoes of the art of the grotto are to be found in the middle of the big city, in the ghastly dripstone formations on the staircases of aging nightclubs, and framing the stages of dusty music halls.

The sober and sensible Friedrich Wilhelm I was chagrined by his forebears' paradise of parterres and cottages. He called it 'tomfoolery', and turned the orangery into a carpet factory with a sort of trading floor on the top storey, and the flower parterres into a military parade ground for his infantrymen. Since no one parades here anymore, the general public can congregate here for their meetings. You can imagine communists demonstrating with flags and pennants and making their encampments. A red Pentecost; they've come from afar, from every part of Germany. The textile proletariat from the Ore Mountains, miners from the pits of Hamm and the cannon-producing city of Essen, which has become a stronghold of the red front, and the Rote

Marine of the Alliance of Red Front-Fighters[43] has come from the North Sea coast. They've also come from the more distant parts of Europe, and the rest of the big wide world has sent its representatives as well; the Defensive Front of the Swiss Labour Force,[44] a Czech worker's resistance group hoisting flags and placards. The Soviet standard is saluted with reverence. Long processions marched here from all corners of the cities, led by strange instruments: trumpets with multiple bells, jazz tubas, African drums. These fighters are uniformed just like those they would like to oust. The grey shirts and brown tunics are belted in military style. And the processions are now orchestrated by the red armbands of the leading pivots, just like the fraternity leaders' galloons in days gone by. In white collared shirts with fluttering red bow ties, they've scaled the sides of their truck, which bears a sign demanding an end to the degrading abuse.

I once accompanied such a procession from the Bülow promenade in the southwest down Yorkstraße, under the railroad crossing whose iron bridge echoed 'Red Front!' and 'Be prepared!' back at us. Old men and women looked down peevishly at these feisty folk from their middle-class, tacked-on balconies. Perhaps they were retired civil servants who hadn't 'adjusted' to the new times yet. But red flags waved from the buildings on the side street, and a few boys joined us on bicycles with their wheels wrapped in red. It went on like that up the shores of the Planufer, across the bridge over the canal, and into

---

43 The Alliance of Red Front-Fighters (Roter Frontkämpferbund) held an important annual meeting on Pentecost.

44 Schutzwehr der Schweizer Arbeiterschaft.

the old city. On Alte Jakobstraße, a grizzled woman stood on a roof terrace, hair in the wind, like one of the Fates of antiquity or a Fury of this new zeal. Younger women lay about in Sunday-fashion with their bare arms on their window cushions, enjoying the music and crowds like in the olden days when companies of soldiers were on the march. In the commercial buildings on Markgrafenstraße, not a soul was in sight. Except on top of one high roof, a figure was moving, and waved with a tiny pennant. On Oberwallstraße, the procession drifted through the silence of the archway, which seals the Crown Princesses' Palace against any trace of the present, protecting its languorous driveway and the old balconies and mansard windows. The procession pushed through this gate in order to meet with the processions from the other suburbs on the square in front of the armoury.

An immeasurably vast crowd filled the whole Lustgarten and Schloßfreiheit square in small groups and processions, from the Palace Bridge up to the Kaiser Wilhelm Bridge. Red banners wrapped along the bars in front of the palace, behind which both the bronze statues of the Dutch princes and Admiral Coligny were nearly rendered invisible, as were the two liberal horsemen, concealed by the fiery letters. On the first steps in front of the cathedral stood a speaker whose declaratory closing speech was repeated by the throng down below like believers repeating the priest's words in the litany. The masses were encamped all around the pedestal of the monument to Friedrich Wilhelm the Just (who apprehensively steps forward into the air), around the granite bowls, on the steps of the museum under the Amazon fending off the tiger, and under the lion fighter. And the monuments looked down upon the many processions wandering back and forth with their flags and placards and effigies lampooning the League of Nations, and across at the groups convening at the Kaiser Wilhelm national monument on the Schloßfreiheit square.

The tour guide doesn't spare us the cathedral, which I avoid viewing insofar as possible, and for a terrible half a minute he pauses in front of it and calls it 'very pretty, especially inside'. But my consolation has just appeared at the curb in the form of a dainty little vehicle. Two levels of glass panes are balanced on pram wheels. Inside are machines made of glinting nickel, and little cups and spoons. An ice-cream vendor: an adorable miniature enterprise glittering like Snow White's coffin.

A glance across the water at the Berlin Stock Exchange building on Burgstraße. People find the same faults with the National Bank building as with these 'renaissance forms'. It's the first building made of sandstone in the newer part of Berlin. For us, the interior of the building is considerably more interesting than its architecture and style. Once, I was permitted to look down from the gallery into the three great halls where the merchants of Berlin were gathered at midday. I saw the certified brokers at their cabinets, the wild swarm that rallied around its more active members, the gestures of selling and buying, raised hands waving the 'asking price', fingers pointing to signal amounts of money. I saw the niches and the long benches, the tables in the smaller and much livelier room for commercial stocks, the calmer room for the banks, and in the one for grain I saw the bags and little blue boxes with samples of rye and wheat in the hands of the traders. You could look down for hours on that sea of bald heads, restless shoulders, waving hands; on the fateful numbers on the boards that seem to fall and fall only, on the yellow and blue lights flashing a special signal in the corners. Peddlers and beggars of all kinds wait in front of the doors to Burgstraße; based on the manner in which the exiting business magnates react to their presence, one could conclude whether business was good or bad that day.

Let's now take a look at a Berlin landmark not listed in any guidebook. I'm talking about the thing down there in the water, by the bank of the Spree, near the arsenal: a tethered barge. I just noticed it for the first time recently. I happened to wander by and saw a couple of street urchins standing on the wooden dock leading to the barge. They wanted to see the big whale that supposedly had been housed in the barge for many years. When I was these boys' age, I was also very curious to know if there was really a big whale inside, but no one ever allowed me to satisfy my curiosity. Which is why I took the youngsters to the register. It was very cheap, and I got a pamphlet for free, a particularly pretty one that I recommend to every visitor and even to enthusiasts of old block printing. Its title page reads: 'The largest mammal in the world and its capture. 22m 56cm long, completely odourlessly preserved. Published by the management of the whale exhibition.' Isn't that a tremendous way to begin? Then we learned that this colossus has warm red blood like us and gives birth to live young 'which are nursed by the mother and defended by her with self-sacrifice at the risk of her own life'. It lies there, preserved using a completely new method, looking as if it were made of papier-mâché, smelling not one mite of blubber though a good deal of barge. You'd like to touch it to convince yourself it isn't really cardboard. But it's written there: 'No touching! Poisonous!' For a while, we look down its throat and at the famed baleen, from which, we learn, whalebone is harvested. Then we enter the special exhibition, where the individual components of the leviathan have been disembowelled and made accessible for us, the general public, to study. For example, there's the throat sack where the animal can store two to three tons of herring. 'For' — as the pamphlet says — 'securing enough sustenance plays a key role for such an enormous animal.' In a separate case, we get to see a tail fin, which — again according to the pamphlet — inspired the invention of the steam turbine. And along with the cartilage, rear fins, ears, and eyes of the whale, there are other sea animals to see, including a few that are simply asking to be turned into nonsense poems: for example, the sea cucumber, sea cow, or the box fish.

I have my reasons for describing this unusual whale exhibition so extensively: I don't trust myself to say anything at all about the neighbouring arsenal.[45] It's too perfect for praise. It is Prussian and baroque, completely Berlinesque and yet fantastical. Well-arranged elements and beautifully implemented decoration, a broad victory facade and delicate trophies. Schlüter's panoply on the balustrade is magnificent, as are the keystones over the window arches. On all four sides of the exterior, he placed helmets that are living representatives

---

45   Today, home to the German Historical Museum.

of the antique, and inside, in the atrium, there are the heads of dying warriors whose grisly death grimaces ornament the sculpted keystones.

For those who are interested in weaponry and war, the oldest cannons are to be found in the dim halls, under the bays of the vaulted ceiling, along with Arabian sabres, gaudy armour for man and horse, standards, uniforms of generals and kings, Zieten's sable caps and panther skins, and Friedrich the Great's last military garb.

The former Crown Prince's Palace across from the arsenal is not a pleasant sight from the outside. Tall columns bear a wide balcony, which makes the stories below it look low and squat, especially when it's viewed from within such a well-proportioned structure as the arsenal. And it doesn't help to know that this palace was once in better condition, and that it entered its current state in the 1850s when it was renovated for the crown prince, later Kaiser Friedrich III. But since it doesn't lodge any princes anymore, it now fulfils a noble purpose. The modern collection of the National Gallery is housed here. And, in my role as a guide for foreigners, I'll just point out the Berlin-specific items: you'll find many admirable cityscapes, along with Berlin history and Brandenburg landscapes, in the countless sheets of the Menzel portfolios, in some of Liebermann's paintings, those of Lesser Ury, and some younger artists. There are also portraits of prominent Berliners in the extensive collection of impressionist and contemporary paintings.

One side of the palace abuts Schinkelplatz, on whose southern side a more attractive building houses another part of the National Gallery on its upper floor. It's the large portrait collection, whose painters and paintings represent a good part of Berlin's artistic and cultural history. The building that harbours this treasure is the Bauakademie, which Schinkel built in red brick with beautifully inset terracotta, and inhabited during the final years of his life. The square in front of the academy is named after this master, and besides his statue there are two other bronze ones — a 'founding figure of science-based agriculture' and a moneyed industrialist, men whose monikers we semi-educated folk recognise mainly from street names, which is why I'm reluctant to even give them here. But you must look at the reliefs on their pedestals. There you'll find curious textbook examples of this truly Berlin mixture of classicism and realism — antiquated machines and gentlemen in toga-esque frock coats.

The Neue Wache, the guardhouse that no one guards anymore except for two statues, is Schinkel's beautiful 'Roman castrum', with heavy Doric columns. Inside, it's empty now — only the classic rifle stands are left — all monument and antiquity. It's better that way, but some Berliners think back with a certain melancholy to the time when the guards paraded. As long as we're at the Neue Wache anyway, let's take a look at the small temple of art over there, half hidden in the foliage. That's the Singakademie,[46] atelier of the master-builder-turned-master-musician Carl Friedrich Zelter — he was a friend of Goethe's. The little bust in the green patch in front of the building is Zelter's mentor and the founder of the musical society from

---

46 Today, the building of the Singakademie is home to the Maxim Gorki Theater.

which the Singakademie emerged. But that was long before it occupied this beautiful building that is somehow out of the way in the middle of the city. Much of Berlin's musical history during the era of Zelter and Mendelssohn is connected to this society and its artistic abode hidden behind the bushes. More than that, it's a slice of life from the best Berlin society that had ever existed, which in the first decades of the 19th century was limited to the rather narrowly circumscribed lives of bourgeois people, in whose family registers the best painters daubed landscapes, and the best poets wrote verse in dainty script. To be a connoisseur of all arts, a dilettante in the best old sense of the word, was a pleasant, pointless, ardent custom that may have bordered on the sentimental-comic from time to time, but nonetheless contributed to the city's unity of feeling and conduct, and, consequently, to its identity.

During this period, the neighbouring building (the former palace of Prince Heinrich, brother of Friedrich the Great) was turned into the university. And the Humboldt brothers seated comfortably before it in their marble armchairs raised the intellectual and scientific aspirations of Berlin society, with their work conducted both in this very place and on distant horizons, those of the Romance languages and overseas.

The building forms the northern end of what is now known as Kaiser Franz Joseph Platz, the square once called 'Forum Fridericianum'.[47] The square's southern half is flanked by the old library — now the university auditorium — and the opera house. Friedrich's master builder, the great Knobelsdorff, had something

---

47 Now known as Bebelplatz.

more beautiful in mind for this palace than what was actually built. Across from his opera house, he wanted to construct a similar temple-palace, making the entire northern half of the square just as monumental as his opera. Though his big plans were never carried out, something impressive nevertheless did come into being under the supervision of Boumann the elder. But that palace remained mostly deserted, for the prince didn't like Berlin and preferred to stay in his Rheinsberg solitude.[48] In 1810, the Friedrich Wilhelm University[49] was founded here, and its first president, chosen by the senate, was Fichte. The three hundred students in its first class grew to over ten thousand with time. We shall reserve judgement as to whether science benefited much from this increase, though I will add humbly that two or three decades ago it was more pleasant to hang around halls of the old alma mater than it is today. Back then there weren't as many exam fanatics. And the front garden wasn't stuffed as full of bronze and marble men possessing neither the dignity of the two Humboldts out front nor the verve of the statues of Savigny and Fichte before the auditorium. This building, once a library, is supposed to have been commissioned by Friedrich the Great in emulation of a Viennese model, with a facade designed by the great Fischer von Erlach. In the vernacular, it's known as 'The Old Wardrobe', because a dubious anecdote claims that the king gave his master builders an ornate piece of rococo furniture as a model.

---

48 The palace of Prince Heinrich of Prussia at Unter den Linden 6 is now the main building of Humboldt University.

49 Known as Humboldt University since 1949.

There's a similar story told about Hedwig's Cathedral behind the square, which is round like the Pantheon: the Catholics of Berlin came to Old Fritz and asked him to build a beautiful church for them in Berlin. The king was sitting at breakfast just then, in a good mood and feeling 'affectionate'. When they asked him what the church would look like, Friedrich took his coffee cup, turned it over, and said, 'It shall look like this.' And so it was that the master builder made the church completely round, and set a round cupola on top of it. The lamp and the cross that we see on the cupola today were added in the 1880s. Its wonderful green patina also appeared at that time, one of the warmest patches of colour on Berlin's still somewhat grey face.

Our opera, Knobelsdorff's masterpiece, has been changed in all sorts of ways by time and human intervention, and not always to its advantage. But we can delight in the fact that the hideous staircase was gotten rid of during the last renovation. The final owner in the imperial era added the stairs to the exterior in the case of a fire, and as Mackowsky[50] said, they gave 'the elegant building the appearance of a dummy constructed for fire-fighting exercises'.

The 'wardrobe' stands wall-to-wall with the palace of Kaiser Wilhelm I, a modest castle fit for a prince. Even in his youth, Wilhelm I kept a frugal house, and when this building was renovated in the 1830s from an old private palace, the master builder had to avoid any unnecessary expense. Since it has always been said that it really isn't much to look at inside, I never went in, until recently I read Laforgue's Berlin

---

50 German art historian Hans Mackowsky (1871–1938).

chronicles. He creates such a nice impression of the silence in these rooms, which were occupied only by the royal couple and half a dozen ladies-in-waiting. The rest of the court was housed in the big palace, in the Crown Princesses' Palace, and in the neighbouring Dutch Palace. When Laforgue entered in the morning to present himself to the empress and read to her, he heard only the ticking of the clocks and the trickling of water in the conservatory. And the silence carried through the whole day, broken only for a minute at a time by the clicking of spurs accompanying a military servant entering with an announcement. While there, he read the royal lady the most important tidbits from the Parisian newspapers *Le Temps*, *Les Débats*, *Figaro*, and *Revue des deux Mondes*, along with excerpts from novels and memoirs. He rarely saw the Kaiser. The royal couple lived more or less separately under the same roof. From the ladies-in-waiting, he learned that the old lord was 'a darling' who cared for and respected his wife and her delicate nerves as if she were a saint. When they had differences, and Kaiserin Auguste's mood grew stormy, Wilhelm was in the habit of saying sympathetically, 'Her Russian blood is agitated once again.' But she was generally at ease, brushing her long pale hand along her brow. The elderly lady was very dignified and not at all popular. Berliners said, 'She's not from around here.' Laforgue's comments made me curious about the interior of the old couple's home, and so recently I went in, along with a batch of other observers.

Yes, it really was there, the office with the historic corner window where the Kaiser appeared when the guardsmen were passing by outside. Supposedly each time he heard the music approaching, even mid-conversation, he buttoned his overcoat across his white vest and straightened his Pour le Mérite order between the lapels of his uniform according to regulation. It is the same military decoration that we see in many portraits of his contemporaries. It cuts a good figure at the throats of all of these distinguished men, whose severe good posture is hardly achievable today. One of them, it's said, avoided leaning against the backrest of his chair until just before his death, explaining to his kin that it could turn into a bad habit. Similarly, the old king held himself upright among all of the uncomfortable furniture that overfills his office. It has been maintained in precisely the condition he left it when he died a few doors down in a modest room facing the courtyard in the dim shadow of the neighbouring building. The tables, étagères, Vertikos, chair, and sofa are all covered in mementos, portfolios, and books. The old lord kept all of this close around him, and oriented himself within it with conscientious precision.

Rarely has a mortal being received so many gifts, framed items, paperweights, such a quantity of worthless and tasteless photographs, vases, pillows, and figurines as this friendly old fogey did, and he kept everything with a deference that is touching. When the table and walls could no longer accommodate anything else, he simply made piles on the floor that stand there today.

On the ledge in front of the bookshelf are photographs of masked family members at a party, an intimate masquerade ball for good bourgeois families. The Kaiser's second breakfast was served on that same ledge, where he ate while standing. A narrow spiral staircase leads from the library into the upper rooms. Wilhelm I climbed these onerous steps far into old age in order to access his wife's apartments. We took a longer, easier route through the meeting room. Bismarck must once have sat in one of the uncomfortable chairs with a Prussian eagle stamped on the back, turning his masters into loyal servants of his politics. We entered the marble staircase where two Victorias by Rauch[51] raise their wreaths, peaceful-looking goddesses of wars long since passed. The Kaiserin's rooms up above are more welcoming and luxurious. Even when she was a princess, Auguste had taken a great interest in interior furnishings, and it is said that she wished to be a decorator. We outsiders wandered rather apathetically past the prestige and comfort of these bright rooms, past the malachite and alabaster of the typical Russian souvenirs, looking out the window frequently, and only snapped back to attention when someone demonstrated the echo in the ballroom to us, which was built into this space as a matter of coincidence, which is to say by accident. One member of our herd made timid attempts to conjure it himself, which our guide allowed with a smile.

Our tour guide dismissed this noteworthy building with a few words, in order to describe more extensively the 'judicious baroque forms' of the massive new national library across the way. Above the entryway, between one bewigged and one bareheaded forefather, there is a bust of the last

---

51   Christian Daniel Rauch (1777–1857), the most prominent German neoclassical sculptor.

Hohenzollern prince with a twirled marble moustache. Inside are an unbelievable number of books, and a large collection of manuscripts, music and map departments, and gramophone records in two hundred languages from every institute imaginable. You can look at everything; but best of all is to sit behind a wall of books in the circular reading room and observe all the gals and fellows studying, taking notes, taking breakfast, and daydreaming in concentric rings around the empty centre.

Ah, breakfast! We've arrived back by the statue of Old Fritz, our point of departure. Why don't we head over to Habel's old-fashioned wine tavern in the lovely hundred-year-old building and have a seat at one of the bald-scoured tables to study the extensive wine menu? Sadly, we're driving on, our journey isn't completed yet. We can only cast a quick, longing gaze at the vases, masks, and grape leaves of the relief over the door.

The street Unter den Linden is still the heart and centre of the capital city, with its four rows of trees, pretty shops, embassies, ministries, and bank buildings — to do it complete justice and to experience its present as well as its past, you would have to conjure up all of its epochs, ever since the Great Elector laid it out as a suburban avenue leading to his hunting grounds, the Tiergarten. You must read about Old Fritz's era in Friedrich Nicolai's[52] superb descriptions of Berlin and Potsdam, capital city and seat of royal power. He records every building on the street, inns such as Stadt Rom, which later became Hotel de Rome on the corner of Stallgasse, now known as

---

52 Friedrich Nicolai (1733–1811) was a famed Berlin bookseller and author, and a principal figure of the 'Berlin Enlightenment'.

Charlottenstraße. Office buildings and businesses recently had to make room for its majestic renovation. He writes of palaces like the Margrave von Brandenburg-Schwedt's — including a list of all of its previous owners — which later became the old Kaiser's palace; or that of Princess Amalia of Prussia, Abbess of Quedlinburg, near Wilhelmstraße where the Russian Embassy is now located; or the one belonging to a certain von Rochow, or a certain Count Podewils; and so on. Then you'd have to take a look at the famous Linden frieze at Märkisches Museum, which captures all of the buildings on Unter den Linden in the year 1820. Now add to that the image of the present, including the driveways for the Bristol and Adlon hotels (whose renovation ousted the magnificent Redern Palace), the stately Ministry of Culture, and the many well-preserved older buildings that house long-renowned shops and office buildings. Maybe you'll come away with the same impression as Varnhagen, who noted after taking a walk down Unter den Linden to the Brandenburg Gate and back: 'The sight awakened a wonderful series of images in me, of the past and the future, a marvellous historical development which carried the little ship of my own being on its churning sea.'

The degree to which the character of our esteemed main concourse has remained the same or changed is a question best left to experienced researchers of the history of social customs, allowing us to examine the present with the naked eye.

The curious foreigner will above all take an interest in the famous intersection with Friedrichstraße, posing questions about Cafe Bauer and Kranzler. Now, Bauer is no longer called

Bauer, but simply Cafe Unter den Linden; its plucky Dionysian and Elysian murals have disappeared, and to be honest, there's 'more going on' in Cafe König across the street; by which I don't mean to critique the comforts of a sojourn in Cafe Unter den Linden — to the contrary! And Kranzler? It still has those curious little iron stakes and chains that the elegant officers from the old Gensd'armes regiments let hang down next to their tight pants-legs in the days of Queen Luise, but since the last renovation, it's lost its old cachet, by which, again, I mean no criticism of its cakes.

You, foreigner, cast a fervent glance down Friedrichstraße, but I don't want to tell you anything about it yet. You'll have to wait for an evening walk before you experience its aged, ever-ageing yet animated secrets and its observable mysteries.

But I'll gladly lead you a few steps past the gateway, off little Mauerstraße. Once you've entered this world of stone, which is more a passageway than a street — the arches of the gate and above them the rotunda, the balcony railings, the glass corridor, the light grey and 'café au lait' of all of the neighbouring buildings — you're in an image of the unadulterated past. The arched gateway on the other side leads to the 'headquarters of the German monetary transfer system', Mauerstraße, and its neighbouring streets. Most significantly, you'll find the massive Deutsche Bank buildings, which are connected to each other with modern-day Bridges of Sighs.

We pass small, genteel-looking buildings with classical window frames, well preserved between their younger neighbours, and rows of beautiful private cars before the hotel and in the middle of the divided roadway, to arrive at Pariser Platz. This square — with the gate at one end, the modest palace's receding facades, and the refreshing green grass to the right and the left — safeguards a silence and a self-contained nature that the noise and bustle surging about it cannot disrupt. The unified tranquillity of the buildings is soothing, interrupted only a little by the Friedländer palace,[53] while the baroque French embassy blends right in. And it's nice to know that here, next to the academies and embassies, the well-to-do and the nobility, a painter and a poet make their homes.[54]

We circle the plaza in front of the gate. Please don't look at the marble balustrades, benches, fountains, and princely statues bequeathed to us by the Wilhelmine architects and master builders. Take this garish white before the serene green Tiergarten for nothing more than a glaring insult to the eyes! God help us, may the Kaiser-couple Friedrich III and his spouse Victoria be removed by the next time you return to Berlin. Look instead at the pretty trees and bushes along the avenue. But soon that irritating, harsh marble comes shimmering through the green again as we head down Siegesallee. Yes, here to the right and left there are thirty-two Brandenburg-Prussian rulers, and behind each of them a marble bench, and on each bench sits — no, no one can sit there, it's too cold — but perched on each backrest are two busts of contemporaries of the ruler in

---

53 Not a palace in the traditional sense, this magnificent building was built and occupied by Jewish industrial baron Fritz von Friedländer-Fuld.

54 Hessel is surely referring to the impressionist painter Max Liebermann. In their notes to Hessel's collected works, Hartmut Vollmer and Bernd Witte speculate that the poet Hessel refers to is Karl Vollmoeller.

question. There's no avoiding it: our car drives remorselessly past the entire set, and each one is named. The question is whether we can manage to have all of these removed before the next time you visit. Berlin is very capable, after all, when it comes to clearing things away, but marble isn't worth much when it's already carved. Still, we must be able to sell it somehow. Thirty-two rulers plus benches and contemporaries! I don't know where to begin. But maybe you'll get an idea of how beautiful this avenue up to the good old Victory Column once was. So, now we've covered the one side, up to Friedrich Irontooth.[55] Here we are at Kemperplatz, and this is supposed to be Berlin's new Roland statue, since we don't have the old one anymore. We could enter the somewhat ostentatious Cafe Schottenhaml here on the corner (the name calls to mind something cosily Munich-esque) and then admire the porcelain collection located up above, old samples from the Royal Porcelain Factory. But our car makes a turn and finishes off the remaining sixteen of the thirty-two. We cast a glance at Otto the Lazy, the only one of these gentlemen to enjoy any degree of popularity, as he had such a nice, sullen way of carrying out his civic duties.[56] And now just sit tight until we come to the Victory Column![57] It's not exactly beautiful, no,

---

55 Nickname for Friedrich II, Elector of Brandenburg.

56 Otto the Lazy neglected his duties as joint Elector of Brandenburg, and received a large financial compensation from the emperor in 1373 in exchange for his resignation. The statue became the butt of jokes when it was included in the Siegesallee series, and seems to have been cemented in popular humour by an 1899 cartoon of it sleeping on its marble bench.

57 Until 1939, the Victory Column stood at Königsplatz in front of the Reichstag, not in the Großer Stern intersection where it is located today.

you couldn't say that. But the tall shaft of the column decorated with cannon barrels is reminiscent of the plant known as a 'horsetail'. And horsetails are beautiful. And the whole thing now belongs to Berlin's garden of monuments. You must admit, despite the cannons, that the column is relatively inoffensive. Oh, and if you love panoramic views, there's one up top with a Baedeker star. You can see the whole Tiergarten toward the south and west, and Moabit to the north, and to the east beyond the dome of the Reichstag you can have another look across the whole old city with its domes and towers, which we saw up close today.

Less harmless, even depicted in Begas's hasty pathos, is the giant on the red granite pedestal.[58] Confident in his headstrong achievement, the bronze cavalryman, his fist on the proclamation of the German Empire, gazes into the distance, across everything he's accomplished, and everything those who came after him did not achieve. He takes no notice of the folk gathered on his pedestal: Atlas with the globe, Siegfried from the opera forging the sword of the Reich, and the two ladies who symbolise the wisdom and power of the nation. The massive Reichstag building behind him seems to be hunched under its domes and towers. The dome of the Reichstag, by the way, isn't nearly as high as Wallot, the master builder, had planned. But even as it is, this enormous crouching animal has a massive beauty all its own, and it represents a mighty feat for the era that produced it.

---

58 Hessel is referring to the Bismarck Memorial, which once stood next to the Victory Column at Königsplatz. Today, it is also located at the Großer Stern.

If you're pining for windows with Reich eagles on them, murals of cities and landscapes, cardinal virtues, marble and bronze Kaisers, stamped leather upholstery with all of the refinement of an International dining car, 'sumptuous Renaissance jewellery', and allegorical ladies, then take a tour of the lobby, reading rooms, large meeting room, refreshment room, foyers, and committee rooms. It'll take you three quarters of an hour. If you have friends among the legislators or members of the press, have them procure a seat in the gallery for you, and attend a session. But if you do, you must be careful not to confuse right with left. It's like with certain stage directions that are intended from the point of view of the actor and not the audience. Orient yourself properly so that you don't mistake the communists for the nationalists and vice versa. You'll be able to pick out our great and minor politicians from newspaper pictures, weekly theatre newsreels, and caricatures; that's always a good time. I also recommend that you read selected pages of Eugen Szatmari's Berlin book.[59] That will give you a brisk introduction to this world where I myself always feel a bit foreign.

We drive on across a bridge over the Spree again and arrive at the 'tents'. Big garden restaurants are popping up there now, where there really *did* used to be tents. Old Fritz permitted members of a French colony to pitch canvas tents here and sell refreshments to the people out walking. Later, there was

---

59 Eugen Szatmari was a Hungarian journalist who wrote in German. The book referenced here is *Das Buch von Berlin (Was nicht im Baedeker steht)* [The Berlin Book (What You Won't Find in Baedeker)].

a stage here where musicians performed. In the days of the 1848 March Revolution, the revolutionaries gathered around the stage, debating how to address the king, freedom of press and speech, popular representation, and so on. For a while they were left to their own devices, albeit surrounded by squadrons of cavaliers. Things were still proceeding with judgement and restraint. Varnhagen reports of reticent masses who returned peacefully from the tents in the dark of night, through the Brandenburg Gate and into the city. And in the November Revolution of 1918, silent crowds also advanced along the gardens of the big restaurants, and once again the tents were the site of a cautiously moderate revolution. But, in general, what is to be found here is peaceful bourgeois relaxation, with music, performances, dancing, and massive platters of 'tent pots' and 'set meals', or a packed dinner. The dancing is pretty tame; even the performances are harmless. And so, to this day, in the middle of the city, there's a restful getaway for an endless number of Berlin's petit-bourgeois families, groups, and clubs. The most beautiful bit of quiet Berlin is the street that leads up to the restaurants on the edge of the Tiergarten. But that's not something you can see just driving by — you have to experience it in the morning and at night. Life here is more old-fashioned and homely than in the beautiful, well-known streets at the southern edge of the Tiergarten.

Our car darts with dreadful speed along the Spree, past the gardens and the Bellevue Palace to the Großer Stern intersection; before, you used to peer through the fence to see if the little princelings were out on a walk. Now, you can ramble along the old garden's alleys, look into the round ground-level room in the side building and imagine the royal summer parties there, decipher the garden tombstones, and gaze over at the old-Berlin street known as Brückenallee, where elderly ladies' flowers linger on weathered balconies. In his final years, depressive if epicurean Friedrich Wilhelm IV often sat on the palace terrace facing the garden, perhaps drafting one of the landscaping leaflets that you can see in the Hohenzollern Museum, receiving his ministers (who had their concerns about his emotional state), and dreaming of his lost empire, in which 'no mere piece of paper should ever come between me and my people', while liberal Berliners grappled with the parliament and freedom.

In the days of Friedrich the Great, Knobelsdorff, master builder of Sanssouci, had a dairy and country house here. And after his death, it was passed down through various hands until it finally fell to Prince Ferdinand, Friedrich's younger brother, whose palace was built by Boumann the Younger;[60] but the dainty pavilion with the Corinthian columns is Schinkel's work.

At Großer Stern, we pass the Saint Hubertus fountain and the hunting figures,[61] dutiful bronze you can't really say anything against, though I try to imagine this square in olden times, when real guardians stood here at this crossing of hunting paths, garden gods who later watched over fashionable society's boulevard. Oh,

---

60 Bellevue Palace was designed by Michael Philipp Boumann and completed in 1786.

61 The fountain, by Cuno von Uechtritz-Steinkirch, was dismantled by the National Socialists and its Hubertus statue lost; the four hunting figures by other sculptors can still be seen near the Großer Stern.

many Berlin Tiergartens and Große Sterns have existed before this one whose roundabout traffic roars through now, and where until recently, as a symbol of this brighter Berlin, a tower of lights once glared.[62]

On the drive up Charlottenburger Chaussee,[63] I quickly point out to the foreigners the way to the old Charlottenhof garden restaurant. It was once a pretty private house, and now it's one of the few inviting cafes in Tiergarten itself. Somehow the Berliners haven't yet cultivated luxury and comfort in their illuminated greenery. What Paris would have made of such well-situated clearings, like this Charlottenhof or the little inn by the boat-landing on the lake!

At the Tiergarten Station, you'll find a small display of the bowls and plates exhibited there by the Porcelain Company; I urge you to dedicate a few of your free hours to visiting the nearby factory. That's a piece from the best of old Berlin. Next to a quiet stretch of the river, a street named after the private founder, Wegley, branches off and leads to the offices and factory. While the sales and exhibition rooms on Leipziger Straße are known to the general public, this out-of-the-way complex with its museum is not as well-known and visited as it should be, with all of its halls and rooms where the porcelain is formed, fired, and painted.

We walk through the garden-like courtyard, by the long, plain buildings and through a gateway into the factory, whose

---

62 The Osram company erected a glowing tower at the intersection for the 1928 Week of Lights.

63 Renamed Straße des 17. Juni in 1953.

construction is also of historical interest. There, we receive a tour of the entire path that the porcelain takes, from wet clay to the flower painter's atelier. In the lower clay cellars, an extensive system of troughs separates the solids from the smoothly flowing mass; liquid streams out into boxes where the finer particles are separated from the water. Feldspar is crushed before our eyes, first coarsely in massive edge mills, then finely in tumbling mills, before being added to the alumite. The whole mass continues on, pressed through filters and agitators, the modern version of the old kneading benches. It's run through a roller-conveyor on round tables. They let us watch as the plaster casters and the workers at the potter's wheels go about their business. We visit the lightly warmed drying rooms where the formed objects stay until they're ready for the first firing; the firing chambers of the gas kilns; the storeys-high round kiln; the final firing room; the cooling room; and the workshops where the barrels for glazing stand. A strange underworld that is half oven, half 'message to the forge'.[64] Finally we arrive at the painters, where today they still faithfully and earnestly daub on the traditional flowers with pointed leaves in metallic paint, which transforms when it's fired. They show us plates and bowls in every stage of completion, before and after firing, before and after their stay in the muffle furnace, where a weak heat melts the liquefying agent from the paint.

A friendly librarian leads us into the library and grants us a look at the royal decrees made by Old Fritz, who, as an

---

64 Hessel is referencing the ballad by Schiller, 'Fridolin', or, *The Message to the Forge*.

industrialist, concerned himself with all of the details of his 'Porcellainfabrique'. All briefings of any importance had to be sent directly to him, and he ensured their receipt with his staunch 'reminders'. He was a good salesman and knew how to hock his wares. For example, if Jews wanted to take up residence, open a business, or marry, they had to buy royal china. After he had become very famous, twenty solid life-size apes were foisted on the philosopher Moses Mendelssohn.[65] By presenting large gifts made in his factory, the king spread its fame. The centrepiece that he presented to Empress Catherine II of Russia became world famous. Under the direction of the king, the business grew, new kilns were constantly being erected, and the technical achievements of the early nineteenth century were implemented to the royal factory's benefit. Although it had to endure all of Prussia's economic struggles, its products always retained their artistic quality and unique identity through the years.

A walk through the exhibition halls here will reveal Berliner porcelain to be a faithful reflection of the current inclinations through all stylistic periods — especially when rounded out by a visit to the sales rooms on Leipziger Straße, which owe their new interior design to Bruno Paul and its adornments to him and artists such as E.R. Weiß, Renée Sintenis, Edwin Scharff, and Georg Kolbe. There are the cherubs and the fates of the Rococo period, and allegorical groups such as 'Water' depicted as a shepherdess with a tiny jug, and Cupid as a cavalryman. The New Palace service and the gleaming dark blue Wrocław

---

65   Most sources agree that this is in all likelihood a legend, albeit a popular one.

Royal Palace service feature more picturesque flowers. Then came the beautiful sketch-like bouquets of the Empire, the classical graces, coffee cups whose shapes are based on Greek and Etruscan models, the delicate bisque sculptures based on Schadow's drafts, the busts of Luise, the attractively designed vases by Henkel based on Schinkel's sketches. We are greeted again and again by these familiar forms and figures, in the Berlin City Palace, in Monbijou Palace, in Potsdam, but above all in the items passed down through Berlin families.

At the point where Charlottenburger Chaussee crosses the Landwehr Canal, a somewhat ponderous gatehouse building stands, which is apparently supposed to highlight the fact that another city begins here. It's rather new, and you shouldn't take it at its word. There's just as little proof here as anywhere else that a border exists between Berlin and Charlottenburg. In a sisterly fashion, neighbouring Charlottenburg took on a number of scientific and artistic institutions, for example the Technical University here to our left. With its magnificent columns, cornices, and sculptures, the massive building celebrates a world that really has nothing to do with columns, cornices, and sculptures. In the foyer, a daemon has been cast as a flamboyant bronze monument, like a renaissance hero. A little farther up, Berliner Straße makes a bend that people call 'The Knee'. Fontane said of this Knee, 'today, its curve is utterly unalluring'. It hasn't become any more alluring in the meantime. And its shape dissolves completely in the chaos of cars and trams that traverse the intersection of many streets which cross here. The continuation of Berliner Straße remains the quietest of these streets. Among the newer houses that line its curbs, a number of smaller, older houses are still present from the time when the journey from Berlin to Charlottenburg was a day-trip made with rented horse-drawn carriages. People drove their coaches through the Brandenburg Gate and across real countryside to get here. They rented summer housing in the idyllic homes that lay on the road connecting the capital city with the royal summer residence, created long ago by the first Prussian king in the little village of Lietzow for his spouse, after whom Charlottenburg is named.

Our arrival at the queen's lovely palace[66] was somewhat marred by a big 1905 equestrian monument to Kaiser Friedrich, on pylons with gods and adornments. Tear it down! The square and its amenities are dedicated to the good of the public, after all! Across from the palace are two domed structures that — it's hard to believe — were barracks. They're reminiscent of some unplaceable garden architecture drawn by the romantic Friedrich Wilhelm IV, and their reverential faces look onto Eosander's green dome with the god of dance hovering over it.

In the palace, Queen Luise's beautiful, rather empty Empire-style rooms contain many unoccupied armchairs and delicate tile stoves. In the east wing, which Knobelsdorff added for Friedrich the Great, is a large ballroom called the Golden Gallery. And you'll find even older splendour in the chambers on the garden side, in the chapels and porcelain chambers from the first king. Unfortunately, you have to walk through the whole thing in the wake of a shuffling guide. But foreigner,

---

66   Hessel is describing the Charlottenburg Palace.

you are allowed to walk in the big park unmolested. On the way there, you'll pass through a room with pilasters whose ornate capitals and medallions made of stucco look as if they'll crumble in the next gust of wind. They've looked that way for the past two hundred years. This neglected room is especially full of the past.

In the garden, you'll walk along the pretty front of the palace and past the busts of the Roman Caesars and along the quiet paths to the mausoleum. In its newly expanded form, it is also a very dignified building, but it made an unforgettable impression on anyone who saw the original one based on Schinkel's plans. It was the first of his little temples to death, and it harbours only Queen Luise and her Friedrich Wilhelm in their marble sleep. For their son and daughter-in-law, another resting place should have been devised without meddling with Rauch's masterpiece.[67] In this park, there's also a strange building far beyond the carp pond and near the river: the Belvedere, where in the 1890s, Friedrich Wilhelm II sat at the feet of his 'Countess von Lichtenau'.[68] Fontane visited the interior of the 'odd, heavily beshuttered construction with the four flat balcony-supporting edifices stuck to the sides and the copper spire'. (Today, it is a residence for public servants and thus inaccessible.) He visited the hall-like round room, and the dim chamber where the king evoked the spirits of the departed, who warned him to return to the path of virtue.

---

67 Christian Daniel Rauch sculpted a sarcophagus for Luise in 1810. Erdmann Enke imitated Rauch's work in 1894 when sarcophagi for Wilhelm I and Auguste were placed in the enlarged building.

68 Born Wilhelmine Enke, the Countess was his official mistress.

Today, the spirits, which Fontane also sensed, have been driven out by a rather banal here-and-now, and the past prefers to reside in some of the park's underbrush and paths that stretch away to the west and north.

But our car takes a turn to the south into the newest part of Charlottenburg, on Kaiserdamm up to Reichskanzlerplatz. On Reichsstraße, we glance over and discern the Heerstraße housing estate coming into being behind it. South of Kaiserdamm, we take in the exhibition halls, the great expo centres, the radio hall and tower. The whole street is generously proportioned, beginning at the Brandenburg Gate and leading here and beyond. For good reason is it the pride of the new Berlin. Our return path takes us by the university for music and visual arts on Hardenbergstraße,[69] a unified complex of buildings in appealing sandstone. Then we cross under the city railway viaduct and over to the Kaiser Wilhelm Memorial Church, where our car comes to a halt. The guide explains that this building is one of the most beautiful churches in Germany.

Now, unfortunately, we're standing in broad daylight and you can see it too clearly. Oh, if only one of the true old churches stood here — from a time when one generation handed the fragment of its dreams on to the next for further completion. If only the wild tumult of the roundabout's trams, cars, buses, and crowds echoed against the stony ruins of grey-aged walls and spires, beneath the torsos of angels and the grimaces of devils — then the 'Broadway' of Berlin–Charlottenburg would have a heart, a centre, a significance for its cafes, movie

---

69   Universität der Künste Berlin (Berlin University of the Arts)

theatres, incandescent letters, and scrolling messages. Instead, here stands a textbook example of a 'late Romantic central-plan construction' with its main and side towers, thirty years old and still looking like new, nothing more than a massive traffic obstruction in the centre of the square. Across from the main tower on the one side and the chancel on the other are two similarly romantic buildings by the same architect — may history forget his name. Light from the Capitol, Gloria-Palast, and Ufa am Zoo cinemas must hammer down on this building at night, breaking up some of the ossified school lessons. We older folk sometimes think back on the time when a wonderful tree left over from the old Tiergarten spread its branches here. (Contemporaries of this magnificent tree are still standing today: one on Wichmannstraße, the other on Viktoriastraße.) But it doesn't matter anymore; today is today. Still, if only this cathedral, with its long name, would at least deteriorate and collapse a little ... The way it is, it stands in the middle of the clattering and roaring, utterly unruffled and Prussian, eyes trained on our dear Lord.

And inside? Already in the foyer, which is, apparently, supposed to recall the narthex of a real romantic church, they let loose with the marble figures: as a lad, Wilhelm receives a marble sword from his father, and he rides as a young crown-prince through the battlefield of 1814 behind riflemen on their bellies, who take their marble aim toward the church's inner entryway; he consults with Bismarck and Moltke over a campaign map between stylised flowers, and is seated in marble between son and grandson, all the better to be revered.

Of the many church windows, it can be said that a benefactor is legibly registered under nearly every one. Among them are many princes, but also cities and individual patrons. Until one beautiful day when these inscriptions are blotted out or disappear, for another century their descendants will be able to chafe at the fact that great-granddad and great-grandma sponsored a laughable painted-glass Satan burning next to the peaceful Redeemer. In the great rose window, little painted prophets hoist their banners in emulation of a naive medieval demeanour, and against a gold background on the ceiling mosaics, ambitious people with halos over their heads conduct themselves as Catholically as their Protestant forms will allow. The Redeemer must bless all of this under an electric light. It's on him to take inventory of this genteel stock, along with the statues ringing a baptismal font of precious material, a ring-shaped chandelier with a diameter of 5.5 metres, and an organ with a casing of embossed copper, 80 stops, and 4,800 tones.

So, before the car drives any farther, I'll jump out here, not into the church, but into a romantic cafe. It's late afternoon, and it isn't too full yet. I'm meeting with old friends from Munich and Paris. Drive on without me, you *real* foreigners!

The Animal Palaces

In the 1820s, the royal pheasantry stood 'on one of the paths that led through the Tiergarten toward Charlottenburg (whose utilisation requires special permission and the key to a barrier, for in this way one avoids the tollhouse and the small toll which one must pay oneself)', reported Eberty in his *Childhood Memories of an Old Berliner*. The pheasantry was established by Friedrich the Great in 1742 via his chief master hunter. One hundred years later, its grounds were used to establish the Zoological Garden at the suggestion of the famed zoologist Lichtenstein. Lichtenstein and Alexander von Humboldt suggested to King Friedrich Wilhelm IV that the pheasantry be made accessible to the Berlin public, along with the Potsdam Pfaueninsel's animal population. At that time, the newly founded zoo still lay far outside the city limits, and for families, visiting it was a day trip. Then the city surrounded it on three sides, and only a bit of Tiergarten to the north buffered it from the encroaching buildings. But even though the buildings are sidled up close to it, and the noise of honking, the harsh headlights, and advertisements batter its walls, as soon as you've stepped through the stone entryway, you've entered another world. To say nothing of the animals — who, after all, are the stars of the show — there's a pond that's overgrown with waterlilies and reeds, nicknamed Lake Lucerne, on whose shores summer-fresh breezes blow. On certain mornings in spring, the avenues turn into a promenade of health regimens, as mineral-water drinkers with a glass of Karlsbader in hand walk their salutary circuit. The zoo is also a magnificent children's kingdom. Babies are taken for walks, youngsters frolic on the playgrounds. And on the so-called 'Gossip Avenue', the older kids can learn the basics of flirting to the sound of music; or at least that was the case when I was young.

As for the nature and customs of the animals, so much has already been said and written that I don't dare to add to it; I'd rather talk about the strange dwellings that they occupy in the garden. Now, since they're imprisoned for our pleasure and entertainment, we are anxious to make their prison as homely as possible. When they enter their walled dungeon, they should have the impression that they are crawling into their hole in the ground, their gully, their hollow tree, their nest. The vulture has its eyrie here: a real cliff, with alpine greenery and scrub pine rooted in the crevices. And yet these cliffs are just like stage settings, like props. And like at the puppet theatre, the children stand before the iron bars, behind which the birds of prey are crouched. Oh, in their eyes maybe the vulture's enormous cage is no bigger than the cramped dickybird cage at their window at home. The zoo is just a continuation of a child's playroom anyway. The red-and-yellow stones of the bear enclosure, the white-and-blue aviary, the yellow-and-blue lion house — they remind us of the pieces in a set of building blocks. Along with the stone, wooden, and steel building blocks, there is also a mosaic puzzle, as well as beautiful zoo buildings in the Moorish and Venetian style, and that of the *Thousand and One Nights*.

Among other things, the zoo has the esteemed purpose of expanding upon the zoolatry of antiquity, and so they built the animals a temple: the camel has its mosque. In its honour, though it derives no pleasure from it whatsoever, the white wall is embellished with a completely unused wrought-iron balcony, and a minaret towers over it. The muezzin could say the evening prayer from there after feeding time is over. The ostriches have a real ancient Egyptian temple. When they seesaw out of their doors and into the open air, they're framed by hieroglyphics and statues of pharaohs. Suns of the sacred kingdom float in the keystones above their doors. On the columns of the entryway, dancers move under a border of plant stems, along with zither and flute players, and the god with the head of a sparrowhawk meanders along the wall. In one of the display rooms of their building, which the ostriches themselves never enter, they've been given a mural of the two Colossi of Memnon along the Nile as a reminder of their homeland.

The hippopotamus has its own building. Inside, it is an eerie red shrine where the children shrink back in fear at the gaping spaces between the bars, behind which the uncanny mass wallows about. Seen from the outside, it's a sort of bathhouse made of brick. The behemoth glides effortlessly into its basin like a fat old lady.

Is the Indian elephant interested in the mosaic dragon pictured on the doors to its palace? Does the zebra love its African farmstead, the Cape buffalo its tree-bark palace? The reindeer must at least find it pleasant that the rooftop ornamentation of his home is as forked and branching as his antlers. And the bison are supposed to venerate the totem poles of beaked birds topped with grimacing gods swallowing frogs. For them, the loaf of bread they chew and stamp on is enough, along with their airy home. But I believe that the coquettish guinea pigs are perfect experts regarding their tiny baroque palace. They sniff at its malachite columns, ogle its vaults. And the wading birds are certainly proud of the Japanese magnificence of their home, the doves of their boardinghouse's sliding shutters. They're also proud of their names, under whose guise goes their splendour: monk parakeet, red-billed buffalo weaver, southern boubou, pearl-breasted swallow. But that's a chapter in and of itself …

And what's that empty pagoda over by the llama's well-appointed gully? 'Adults only' is written there, so it's neither for animals, nor for children. The music pavilion is also for adults. Soldiers are locked inside of it during the day and forced to trumpet and drum. At night — as one smart-aleck older cousin informed the children — the flamingos from the neighbouring pond go to sleep in the pavilion.

Sometimes wild peoples, who stay only briefly, live as nomads alongside the home-owning, long-established animals. Somalis in sweeping white cloaks bow their woolly heads over the glowing coals of a campfire and roast freshly slaughtered mutton on a spit. Tripolitanians dance to tambourines. Indians walk dignified, their narrow-calved legs raised high.[1]

The aquarium makes me think of the old one, which was located on a side street of Unter den Linden. A very old uncle whose bachelor's apartment was located nearby took me a few times as a small boy to that building where the animals of the sea lived. And there, where the deep-sea fish swam between algae and coral, animal-like plants and plant-like animals of the viscous, heaving seafloor — precisely there — was a buffet for the visitors. With a frisson of dread, I ate an undersea ham sandwich and my uncle drank a beer that seethed in his glass like the mead that Thor received from the giant, and which actually *was* the sea.

While this old aquatic kingdom had something labyrinthine and cavernous about it, with surprises and adventures (just like the book *Animal Life* by its founder, Brehm), today's aquarium here at the zoo is an upright, clearly structured building whose floors roughly correspond to the three elements water, earth, and air: the ground-floor aquarium, the second-floor terrarium, the third-floor insectarium. And all of the creatures live, swim, and creep in the stone, sand, and plants of their homelands, caught in display cases and glass tanks. A high-ceilinged central

---

1   Hessel is describing a human zoo, in which travelling exhibitions displayed non-Europeans in 'natural settings' alongside animals. The practice began in Berlin in 1878 and continued until the Second World War. Hessel is disappointingly uncritical on the subject. It is worth noting the bitter irony of the fact that at the end of his life, when he was interned in Les Milles concentration camp, he inspired the ire of some of his fellow inmates for refusing to take a critical political stance, even on their own imprisonment. Hessel's apolitical approach, apparent throughout his work and in reports made by contemporaries, can in such cases only be considered a grave flaw.

space is outfitted as a half-dry Nile or Rio Grande, and, from a bamboo bridge, you can watch crocodiles crawl out of the shallow water onto their tropically warm sandy shores. The lizards inhabit their stony waste, the rattlesnakes their dry plot of Brazilian earth. For the boa's greater comfort, artificial southern sunlight is provided. The smallest of the small aren't made to feel any less at home. The Helgoland lobster is housed in real Helgoland stone; the trout in a mountain stream that splashes over rocks. The bee works in its hive — its little home is cemented into an old oven, and a real kitchen table with dirty dinnerware is made available to the cockroach. Cow dung is provided for the scarab, who rolls little round pills out of it, in which its eggs grow to larvae. Sea flora of all kinds are cultivated in undulating fields of algae. There are even sea cucumbers; under the anemones, there's one with wax-white flower petals like a chrysanthemum, which turns into a voraciously wriggling, lengthening creature like magic — certain women could wear them on their dresses instead of those fake flowers.

But the best part is the true realm of the fish, where great catfish probe with their barbels, where the little seahorse nods its delicate armoured head, where changing colours and shifting patterns surpass every artist's fantasy, and whose denizens go by chanchito and cichlid, bleak and silver bream, olm and ide. The aficionado will also find the astounding veiltail goldfish there. With its colourful trailing vestments, this ornamental fish is so genteel that it could not survive out in the world.

Berlin's Boulevard

Tauentzienstraße and Kurfürstendamm have the important cultural task of teaching the Berliner to be a flaneur, unless this urban pastime should at some point become unfashionable. But maybe it's not too late. The flaneur reads the street, and human faces, displays, window dressings, cafe terraces, trains, cars, and trees become letters that yield the words, sentences, and pages of a book that is always new. To correctly play the flaneur, you can't have anything too particular in mind. On the stretch of road between Wittenbergplatz and Halensee, there are now so many possibilities to run errands, eat, drink, to go to a theatre, film, or cabaret, that it's easy to promenade without the risk of developing a set goal, leaving oneself to the unforeseen adventures of the eyes. Glass and artificial light are two great helps, the latter especially when it's combined with a bit of remaining daylight and twilight. Then everything becomes multiple, new nearnesses and distances come into being, the happiest mixture *'où l'indécis au précis se joint'*.[1]

Incandescent advertisements light up and disappear, scroll away and return, altering the height, depth, or shape of their buildings. That's all to the good, especially on the parts of

---

1 From Paul Verlaine's 'Art poétique': 'Where the Wavering and Precise are joined'.

Kurfürstendamm where many dreadful towers, protrusions, and overhangs remain from the darkest days of the private-building boom. Only now do we have the opportunity to crowd them out. These horrid zigzagging additions to the 'mutilated houses' (as we used to call them) disappear behind the new architecture of advertising. In these palaces, the excessively high-ceilinged public rooms face the street, and the dark back rooms are for private life, but we can besiege their facades by installing shops in them, liberally simplifying the ground floor. And there are always new shops, because the department stores open gleaming branches here, which simply absorb the best retail shops. New purposes are invented for glass, metal, and wood, giving colour to the old-Berlin grey and pale yellow. As soon as one of the buildings becomes dilapidated, or even just needs repair, the new architecture shaves every braid and tress from its boyish head, leaving a clear, linear facade. In front of many cafes, the terraces extend far onto the sidewalk, unifying the building with the street. One of them even has a Parisian-style brazier, to sustain this unity in winter.

Our boulevard's increasingly southern lifestyle also displays the rudiments of democratic urban joyousness, as Wilhelm Speyer put it in his new-Berlin novel, *Charlott, a Little Crazy*:

> In the limbs of this once so ungainly city, this city full of protestant national philosophy and military philosophy, a faintly glimmering fire flashes. A will to lightness, especially in the spring and summer months, began to direct the body of the metropolis in its first, increasingly adroit movements. Even the policemen had learned to laugh at confusion. No

longer did they bellow through their bristling moustaches above curling lips. They were enormous figures, gesticulating with their arms raised, disciplined and yet unmilitaristic in the old-fashioned sense. Ever in motion, the free and easy, daily increasing beauty of the women and children of all classes was beyond doubt. Thus, the big city didn't destroy this beauty, but rather awakened it, fostered it, and allowed for its radiant flourishing. In the streets one no longer saw sulking residents with scoured clothing, their excessively starched underclothes also visible. The style of clothing had become less dramatic. It was more democratic and therefore more elegant.

In the new west, it's interesting for the flaneur to observe, or to sense, which direction traffic — or to make it more coarse, more Berlin-esque — *business* increases or dwindles, and how one street sucks the life from the others, or how one part of a single street does so to the neighbouring parts. Tauentzienstraße, which is just a continuation of Kleiststraße, has made the latter empty and quiet. The last bit of Kleiststraße, between Lutherstraße and Wittenbergplatz, is the clear segue. On that segment, you have the feeling of already being on Tauentzienstraße. It can't be because the buildings are more modern; it must be some subterranean law of the city. Lutherstraße has a quiet stretch that reaches just to Augsburger Straße. Beginning there, there's more traffic all around Scala.[2] You can imagine why. On one side of the street, there is a row

---

2   Scala was one of Berlin's most popular variety-show venues between 1920 and 1944.

of private villas with gardens from the old days. But then, why has the opposite side remained so quiet? Kurfürstendamm has taken the traffic away from Kantstraße, which branches off from it at the Memorial Church, and then runs parallel to it at a gradually increasing distance, though Kantstraße remains fairly longitudinal. At first, Kantstraße tries to keep up with it, offering a bit of cinema and theatre, but even before it reaches Savignyplatz, it stops trying to compete and becomes increasingly petit bourgeois. The well-known trend toward the west pushes the growth of commercial and residential districts in one direction, but there are also many other detours. There are routes of development that stall after a short distance, and others that work out. Property and building speculation must be one of the strangest mixtures of luck and instinct.

The Circle Line bridge at the end of Kurfürstendamm leads to the Grunewald colony. But before we reach the villas and gardens there, we pass through a stretch of folksy entertainment venues: cinemas, dance halls, and especially … Luna Park. This noteworthy attraction has everything that is to be found in other big cities' Luna Parks and amusement parks, and it meets the Berliner's particular need for a fairground. And this need is an old one. In his *Old Berlin in the Year 1740*, Ernst Consentius describes the summer establishments on the Spree near what is now Schiffbauerdamm: their hedge mazes, carousels with jousting horses, their swings, nicknamed 'clock reels'. As Consentius explains, these clock reels were 'mighty wooden lions with leather saddles in which one man was seated, pushed back and forth by one or, better, two others until he was propelled so high as to throw five or six balls into a sack tailored to that purpose which stood six cubits or two men high. A lady may also seat herself there and be reeled and pushed *pro lubitu*.' As for the Fortuna game, he reports that it was 'on the ground fashioned of wood, with nine holes, the hole in the middle shall win, for Fortuna is painted o'er it.' The era of the Tivoli beer garden, in Kreuzberg around 1830, is illustrated with many amusing pictures. In them, the circular track known as the 'the Slide' makes its first appearance. Potted topiaries dot the track grounds. The carts have velvet tassels, and a fat Berlin madame sits inside one of them, legs akimbo, crying to her thinner, struggling companion: 'Hold me, Brennecke, my head's a'swimmin'!'[3] And so it has remained, into our day. Anywhere open spaces gape between suburban buildings, a fairground will fill the emptiness for a while with its shooting galleries, wheels of fortune, dance floors made of wooden panels, and big sausage-eating contests.

Here in Luna Park, everything is more modern, and offered on a larger scale. Above the gondola swings, the Iron Sea of bumper cars, the rollercoaster, an enormous firework illuminates the balancing bridge and Lake Halensee with flames — a sight to rival a flaming Treptower or any other fiery amusement park.

There are stalls for hot Vienna 'Lublinchen' sausages. Sellers cry out 'chocolate, biscuits, nut rolls', but you can also dine elegantly on the terrace. All of Berlin comes here: the lowly

---

3   Hessel is likely describing an illustration by the social satirist Alfred Hopf (1815–1885), whose work featured a recurring working-class character named Brennecke.

sales girls and the great ladies, the bourgeoisie and bohemians. Luna Park is 'for everyone'. Since recently, there's also a special attraction there: the big wave pool, where you can splash around until late into the night.

When you've left Lake Halensee behind you and find yourself on the banks of Hubertussee and Hundekehlesee, that's where the colony of beautiful Grunewald mansions begins. The forest sacrificed many of its slender pines for it, and it now stands in the middle of well-tended bushes and beds, with a bit of forest preserved for the sake of memory.

Going to Grunewald used to be a long trek, like an outing to Tegel or Grünau, but now a number of well-to-do and prominent people live there. And the rest of us sometimes go to Grunewald to visit, stepping out of the tram, which rattles along its track in a cumbersome, timid fashion next to the smoothly gliding cars. We walk up and down a few garden-lined streets, and we're admitted into the home of a young artist and art enthusiast for music and tea. His clan has agreeably wed art and banking by marriage and blood for more than a hundred years. Or we enter the evening company of the great publisher who unified the champions of 1890 with those of 1930 in his house.[4]

To find any forest in Grunewald today, you have to go a good distance farther, to Krumme Lanke or to Paulsborn. There you'll find pretty paths for afternoon strolls that will make you properly homesick for a night on the boulevard. And so

---

4 Hessel is referring to Samuel Fischer of S. Fischer Verlag, which published his first book in 1905, *Verlorene Gespielen*. Fischer lived at Erdener Straße 8.

we find our way back from whence we came. Along with the commands to let Elida make us beautiful and to buy Elektroluxe and Frigidaire, billboards admonish us to spend our 'Evenings at Scala'. We obey and make our way to the famed variety-show hall on the border of the new and old west.

When you look up from your seats on the main floor, into the blue and white-clouded sky of the ceiling mural, you'll notice a line of lighter panels which emit dusty funnels that fall onto the artists as pools of light. Flashing metal fixtures hang over the balcony boxes, and frame the edge of the stage like portholes. Once, I visited the man who services all of these lights, the footlights and the chandeliers. Instead of interviewing directors and stars, I sought out the lighting manager and his crew. He received me in his headquarters, next to his control equipment. From there, he turned the footlights and chandeliers on and off by turn. Wires travel out to the variable resistors, as do telephone lines to the lighting captain's team. Then we tiptoed up the steps, first to the resistor chamber, then farther through the wooden chaos of the attic to the 'bridges' — that's what you call the workspaces for the men who helm the spotlights. And while we walked, he described to me how the curtain behind the artists is changed from red to black to ivory depending on their costume and number, how flaws and dark circles under the eyes can be avoided, how the team deliberates at length before each routine and then a dress rehearsal is held for the lighting, during which he sits down below, next to the conductor, telephoning with his crew up above.

Behind the scenes — across the courtyard and beyond an

unkempt garden — you can see our Pantheon, the Wilmersdorf gasometer. And it was there that I found the wise people who oversee the foolish artist-types, the pullers-of-strings who make it seem as if the clown shoots the sphere off the stand. This is the domain of the hands whose work is invisible to the public, which toss and catch the tyres and bottles. Sedate men rein in the performers' too-loud chatter; the girls can have their capers up there on the stage, like children playing outside. And when these children are onstage, they have other managers, who seem to be true actors. They hand the players new implements when they've tired of the one at hand. They use ropes to pull the background curtain apart so that imprudently tossed balls don't bounce against it. These conceited, talented children always overdo things, and when they return — panting, exhausted, sweating — they're dried off and wrapped up by their chaperones.

Also note the self-sacrifice of the helpers and chaperones you *can* see, but who aren't listed in the program. The grotesquely costumed clown musician accompanies a dour gentleman in a business suit. This clown does a few tricks himself that have a certain classic perfection about them, but only for the purpose of accentuating his companion's new tricks. He allows himself to be made the fool, befuddled, tormented, and he always turns to the audience without grumbling, with a pained, proud smile, the motions of his hands unleashing applause for the others. He accompanies the strong woman as her dainty squire, a human workhorse, a drone. Before she gets to work, she dines with him. But it's a curious supper: hardly have they eaten a morsel or drunk a sip, when she's overcome with the desire to lift the table and chairs and to make dumbbells out of everything. The squire, who is clearly no stranger to women's moods, must save the glasses, gather the plates, and keep up appearances for his happy reveller for as long as possible. Before he has the chance to slip up, he's grabbed by the scruff of his neck and whipped in the air, and even then he can't lose his composure and has to keep smiling. Finally he lands way up on the grand piano that the Powerful One has balanced on her bosom, so that she can sing 'Still ruht der See' in a nightingale's voice underneath it. And up top he lays a hand across his ear and harkens like a nymph.

The female helper is all nymph, angel, peri. She stands serenely against the backdrop and waits in a yellow shawl and Turkish pants, pillar and ornament, until the illusionist needs her; he's just placed a young lad in a sword-pierced, sinisterly sealed box. Her expressive face distracts us from his enchantments, which we're not yet allowed to figure out. And this selfless woman doesn't smile in order to please us, but rather so that *he* pleases us. You see, she herself is now the victim and is put in a sorcerer's cauldron, which she steps out of again with a slow smile that fills the artist's silences.

And here comes the woman in equestrian boots! Behind the scenes, she looked after a little poodle that shivered with stage fright. She knows when the impatiently stomping pony should get his sugar, and when he really shouldn't. She brandishes her stool, holds the hoop in the air at just the right moment, and does everything as if it were a pleasure and not a bitter labour whose glory is reaped by the man in the middle cracking the whip. In between, she dances a little number or even does a somersault, and all of it is just decorative, an accompaniment, a spot of colour.

You can't really include the animals among these unnamed minor figures. Since they labour so tamely, they *do* reap a portion of their masters' glory, and perhaps they're ambitious; the sea lions certainly are. I won't venture to guess about the feelings of the ponies, bears, or elephants. As for the monkeys, I believe that they're a bit frustrated about their zoological relatives who have made a better job of it.

There's much to be said of the items used in the variety show: the flashing metal stands and tables; a set of parlour furnishings that sacrifices its refinement to be balanced, thrown, and generally made absurd; the elegant divan that is really just a box from which pirouetting dancers emerge; the tiny velour armchair that resigns itself to being squatted upon by elephants; the gold-plated bedstead that allows a clown to play music on its golden buttons; the crocheted blanket that glasses and knives hop across; the country-style bench that the eccentrics have recently vacated, leaving it empty, as if stuck to the background, while they act in the foreground. And this background itself — the painted candelabra on the parlour wall, the heroic landscape — has the attraction of things ignored, which draw attention to the other purposeful things, in the variety show more than anywhere else.

The Old West

The old west of Berlin — with the exception of the Tiergarten quarter, which has suffered much but nevertheless has come through it — the old west has lost out, as one says of beauties that are no longer fashionable. 'We' no longer live in the old west. Even before the turn of the century, well-to-do families moved out to the area around Kurfürstendamm, and later even farther past Westend or Dahlem, if they couldn't make it all the way to a villa in Grunewald. But some of us who were children in the old west have retained a loyalty to its streets and buildings, which really aren't anything special to look at. To us, it's an experience to walk up one of their front steps, which once led to the homes of friends and relatives. So much memory is caught up in them — in the tasteful staircases with brown wooden railings, colourless walls, and the grey figures etched into the windowpanes, as well as certain palatial staircases where one climbed steeply to a mezzanine level with imitation marble and ostentatious stained glass.

If we're there under some pretext or for some occasion — to view a furnished room, for example — we recognise the old world under the layers of the new: the sliding glass door barricaded behind the shelves which once separated the parlour from the *Berliner Zimmer*,[1] the visibly slanting divan in the shadow of the grand piano, which stood here under a velvet cover with the family photos. Near the window, the tropical world of potted palms remains on a humble plant stand. From the *haut pas* at the window in the *Berliner Zimmer*, we see the pale grass sprouting between the stones in the courtyard, just as it always has. Except that the stable and carriage house that once belonged to the old general in the *piano nobile* has now been replaced by an automotive repair shop.

A few buildings from the old days remain unchanged on side streets of Maaßen, Derfflinger, and Kurfürstenstraße. Their gardens are wonderfully isolated islands. Others have deteriorated despite their gardens, in Karlsbad, for instance, near the Potsdamer Bridge. The fountain there in the greenery has a statue that is crumbling so badly that its debris will soon need clearing away. A similar one in the front garden is still well preserved. It stands before the old family-owned building in the middle of one of the liveliest business districts, Potsdamerstraße near Linkstraße, though a newspaper has hung an enormous sign over the antiquated frieze, and occupied the front rooms of the second storey.

The old west — even the smoke-blackened streets near the train stations still offer up a dove frieze here and there, with the mask of a female face between naked boys with thyrsus staffs over their shoulders crouching on tendrils; an entryway like a

---

1   In a typical Berlin apartment building constructed around a courtyard, the *Berliner Zimmer* is a room located at a corner connecting the front and side wings. They have only one small window facing the courtyard, and so they tend to be cavernous and dark.

temple door. And all of it constructed and moulded in poor or middling materials by the last of the students of Schinkel — the final relics of Prussia's Greek existence.

Before we city kids get to see real antiquities in museums and in foreign lands, we are exposed to a bit of second-hand mythology. In our family homes, there's a bronze Apollo on father's desk that points to the door, or a bust of Venus in the parlour, the marble of her arm-stumps mirrored in the glass; you can't be sure if these strange naked beings are looking toward you or away. When the child goes outside, on the way to school or on a walk, he's sure to encounter more figures in the world that awaits him. Behind the garden fence, a Flora lifts a wreath or a bowl. In the alcove before a door, a Hebe pours something invisible from a jug. On the stairs outside the coal depot, one of the four Graces stands in a clinging pleated dress, her right knee forward — they often seem to be holding or offering something that generally isn't there. We older children of the Berlin west may still remember the muses in a front garden on Magdeburgerstraße. They're gone now. They stood there like ruins of themselves, dutifully raising their sphere or quill for as long as they had hands. They followed our steps with their white stone eyes, and these heathen girls' gazes became a part of us.

Does the bearded Apollo — who once stood at a playground I can no longer locate — still exist somewhere in Tiergarten? We used to throw our ball against his backside where it protruded above the stump supporting him. That may not have been respectful, but it did kindle a certain affection for him.

A handful of sphinxes also lay on our routes: for example, the four on the bridge with their backs to Hercules completing two labours midway across it. Each sphinx carries a child with a cornucopia on its back, and they permit the buses to pass. Both of these labouring Hercules figures are somewhat unsettling. They stand in such a way that they *or* their opponent, the lion or centaur, could fall into the water if things go much further. The sphinxes, on the other hand, are reassuring. They don't reveal their riddles. I know of an even more harmless sphinx over the entryway of a building across from the wall of the Zoological Garden. She waits like a friendly custodian's wife, and she still has her wings and paws. This cat seems to belong to the realm of Kurfürstendamm, and not in the old world in which we wanted to remain.

We find our way back to quieter streets, and the little capitals on the buildings' different storeys remind us of our first lesson in the different kinds of columns, given to us by our father or older brother while on a walk; he taught us to distinguish between the Doric pancakes, the Ionic snails, and the Corinthian chalices with their fourfold leaves. This architectural kindergarten continued with whole colonnades when we made our way down Unter den Linden from the Brandenburg Gate to the opera house and the Neue Wache. But when we arrived at the little gate temples at Leipziger Platz, another interesting discovery awaited us nearby. I'm referring to the eight groups of sandstone figures spread across the grass — they once held the lanterns on a bridge that had long since been destroyed, and they'd ended up here in the greenery. We didn't realise that it was lanterns that they were supposed to be carrying; we were mystified by the way they fussed over their indistinct objects, and over each other. They always interested me far more than the two generals, Count Brandenburg and Count Wrangel, who attempted to draw attention to themselves closer to the street. If I had a voice in city planning, I would remove a whole series of such war heroes and otherwise famous men who seek attention on public squares, bridges, and avenues, and replace them with anonymous garden gods in scant clothing.

Now, until that comes to pass, let us be content with what we have, even if it's just the detail work on old buildings: medallions with girls' heads surrounded by abundant hair or boys' faces under Phrygian caps; little sacrificial or victory processions in bas-relief over the *piano nobile*, and cherubs who turn arabesques in the foliage over the doors, or crouch under the windows. These cherubs were always particularly empathetic figures, because they reminded me of my own boyish body. The ones in front of the old arsenal were exceptionally alluring, standing larger-than-life at the foot of a giantess, while the ones up at the top by her tremendous breasts acted instructively, as they nestled blissfully against the pleated fullness. It's rare that you see such cherubs and goddesses, but there is another kind of mythological person, a whole *plebs deorum*,[2] who commonly accompany us: caryatids and atlantids. A child knows nothing of such obscure names, he just sees girls built into the walls of buildings, carrying a minor burden, wearing their little capitals as crowns. Below the waist, they're nothing but wall. Some of

---

2   A crowd of gods.

them have to bend and exert themselves to hold up overhanging beams. They alternate which arm they use: one uses the right, the next the left, and their free hand rests at their knee. Bearded men haul the building on raised arms and with their necks. Boys brace their shoulders under an arched doorway and reach toward their neighbour, over a lion's head. Some of them have genuinely heavy loads to bear, their abdominal muscles clenched into deep trenches; others seem to exaggerate their effort a little and show off their muscles more than necessary.

While these men and women for the most part carry on their existences out of doors, we are occasionally given the opportunity to see some of them in an enclosed space. When invited to see *The Marksman* or *The Magic Flute*, you spy those whitish friends from your daily walks, ceremoniously holding up the auditorium's parapet. And in another house of culture, there are two more that I've always particularly loved, effortlessly upright under their load, like their models in the temple in Athens. I'm referring to the figures on the great organ at the philharmonic, to the right and left of the filigreed grillwork on that mighty musical radiator. They hold lyres without actually playing them, their hollow stares directed straight ahead. And all of our feelings pour into the empty shells of their faces when the waters of the music carry us up to them. It's true that there are two Christian angels ducked beneath the arched ceiling on burdened wings, nearer to us than these two goddesses. The angels look down on us more obligingly, but we remain faithful to the heathen women.

Tiergarten

A Sunday in autumn. Twilight. A little steam rises from the ground, not as much as from a field, more like that from a potato patch. Lovers are seated on the many benches scattered in the half-darkness and complete darkness along the winding paths. Some of them seem to be a bit unpractised in the art of love. They could learn a thing or two from a Parisian worker caressing his sweetheart. Some of them have claimed a whole bench to be alone together, but even those who have to share a bench with another couple don't seem bothered by the fact.

I'm looking for the bearded Apollo from our childhood playground. In the meantime, I've learned that he's from the eighteenth century, and originally stood at the Potsdam City Palace, then in front of the Brandenburg Gate. It's even mentioned in Baedeker, even if it's only in the fine print. I can't find him and I end up at the Goldfish Pond. I keep my distance from the monument there at the end, with the busts of three musicians in a niche. Instead I walk over to the cherubs ensconced in the natural niche of the bushes. There's Mercury as a little boy, wearing a winged cap and holding a snake staff. He's patting a tiny naked peasant, who seems to be holding a sheaf. Surely that's supposed to symbolise the alliance between commerce and the cultivation of the land. Across from the water's edge, I find a cherub wearing a Prussian Pickelhaube helmet with a sort of bayonet, and a little companion blowing something on the tuba next to him. The two remind me of the tantalising allegorical figures made by the porcelain factory. A third group of figures is missing too many of their arms for me to guess at what they held and signified. They're especially beautiful just as they are.

Down a side path, a little slice of margrave shimmers in front of the Siegesallee. I let its allure remain at a distance, I'm wary of going down to the thirty-two wretched statues with shifting leg positions. Another bush and a sandstone couple, she furnished with flax, he leaning against a wheel. Piloting a ship? Prussian Maritime Trade Company?

Here, the path leads away from the pond to the circle of grass where Tuaillon's Amazons sit tensely, yet at ease, on horses, enlarged replicas of the originals in the National Gallery. They were the first Berlin women whose posture had a gentle corset-less curvature, unlike their royal contemporaries not far from here who, laced up in ever-tightening sheaths, waited by the rose garden for their escorts.

I walk on without any particular direction in mind. I don't know if I'll arrive at Rousseau's island or Luise's. And, by a happy accident, all at once I'm standing in front of the Apollo I haven't been able to find for years. I see him in profile. Moonlight animates the hand with which he grasps his stone lyre. He has an aggressive manner of gripping it, rather than a distinguished classical style. Tradition being what it is, he doesn't need to try to be antique — he can still be baroque, the garden musician of our playground. But he's not on the playground anymore.

Anyway, the maturing half-darkness is overgrown and labyrinthine, just as it was here thirty or forty years ago before the last Kaiser had his nature preserve turned into something more orderly and prestigious. At his command, the underbrush was cleared, many paths were widened, and the lawns were improved, all of which is commendable. But beyond that, the Tiergarten lost much of its special intimate appeal, its charming playroom-like disorder, the snapping of twigs and the rustling of leaves that weren't immediately cleared from the narrow paths. Back then, ponds sometimes sprang up among the dense foliage. As for monuments, there were only a few friendly marble people, such as Herr von Goethe, who looks as if he'll soon be rushing off. He's staying just long enough to try on his admirable cloak, and to be present while some women in Greek garb share a lesson from his poetry with some little boys — or with Friedrich Wilhelm, who looks toward the Luise Island. Supposedly, he looked in that direction even before the construction of the monument to his Luise, which all children love. Experts taught us that the king's figure and garments were made very accurately. Even the patches on the boots of this thrifty monarch, who was known to occasionally don mended footwear, are there.

I'd like to take this opportunity to share some of what I've learned about the history of the Tiergarten. According to a deed from 1527, Crown Prince Joachim the Younger made a gift of the land to the township of Cölln 'for the establishment of a hunting and pleasure garden'. Under the Great Elector, the

Tiergarten, with its large population of game, reached as far as Gendarmenmarkt, and the 'Small Tiergarten' included all of Moabit and the area of Wedding. Gradually, Dorotheenstadt and Friedrichstadt ate into the forest grounds. A broad avenue was constructed to the palace of Queen Sophia Charlotte. And the transformation from a hunting preserve into a leisure park began. The board fence that once enclosed the whole perimeter came down. The Großer Stern intersection was created, as well as the avenues that branch off from it. Friedrich the Second planted trimmed hedges there, and beech trees lashed into pyramids. Over a dozen statues followed after that, not margraves, but Pomonas, Floras, Cereses, Bacchuses, and the like. The people called them *'die Puppen'*, the dolls. And they called the path to them *'bis in die Puppen'*, which became a German idiom meaning 'a very long way' and, eventually 'until late in the night'.

In 1790, the Rousseau Island was created in a marshy part of the park, in accordance with the plans for the site where Jean-Jacques is buried. Our Rousseau Island — we paddled and skated around it, and called it by its name long before we knew whom it was dedicated to. Villas and country houses bordered the park: the inviting home of Jacob Herz Beer, who was Meyerbeer's father; and Iffland's beautiful garden house.[1] Schleiermacher's friend Henriette Herz lived on the nascent Tiergartenstraße. A famed caricature from the era has her out on a stroll in the Tiergarten with Schleiermacher's head in a

---

1   Giacomo Meyerbeer (1791–1864), opera composer. August Wilhelm Iffland (1759–1814), actor and dramatist.

handbag. The caption: 'The things salonniére Herz has in her clutches!' Back then, the park was still a real wilderness; only the 'English' portions were manicured. It wasn't until the 1830s that the Tiergarten was systematically overhauled by Lenné. But he left little bits of wilderness that remained in our childhoods. What I remember most from that time are the tiny, high-arching bridges over the streams that were sometimes guarded by bronze lions, the railing chains hanging from snout to snout.

And the lake known as Neuer See is just as it was back then, or it seems so to me. It's getting too late to head there today, and so in my mind's eye I trace its coves and wooded isles, where we skilfully skated arm in arm, writing figure eights in the ice. In autumn, we stepped into our skiff there, from the bridge in front of the boathouse, with the darling woman who manned the rudder. And later, when we read the famous poem dedicated to a park farther south,

'With our skiff we traced the curve of the horizon
Around a bronze-bowered sprinkling of islands'[2]

we Berlin children thought of our Neuer See.

---

2   From 'Nach der Lese' in *Das jahr der Seele* (1897) by Stefan George.

The Landwehr Canal

It begins and ends in front of factory smokestacks, and it connects the busiest parts of the upper and lower Spree, but on the way it meanders through so much urban idyll that its name has a placid ring in our ears, as if it were still the old Schafgraben, which once flowed along the southern city gates and was known as the 'Green Shore' until the 1880s, before its banks were paved in blocks of stone to make it four full beams in width.

A heavily laden barge glides slowly through its waters. A man with a long pole pushes the boat away from the embankment; a little dog crouches, a fire smokes. Steam rises from the kitchen as if it were a gypsy wagon. Other barges rest along the shore, offering apples for sale, red as the cheeks of mariners' children.

Soon after the canal has left the chemical works and the Charlottenburg Institute of Technology behind it, it is fringed with tree-lined avenues, and for a while its shores are called Gartenufer. Bridges cross it as if they were crossing a garden stream. There's the Lichtenstein Bridge, which leads from the rear entrance of the Zoological Garden to the Tiergarten, not far from the locks, whose glossy surge and crashing foam children love to watch. Looking at the treetops mirrored in the water here, you would hardly believe that this peaceful bridge was once profaned by villains. They threw the dying body of a noble fighter into the water a few paces from here, a woman who had to atone for her goodness and bravery with her life.[1] It's easier to understand the fact that some troubled and forsaken souls have sought death in the beckoning waters of the canal.

At the Cornelius Bridge, the park landscape of the Gartenufer transforms into a city landscape. And the atmosphere in this area, which combines a whiff of park, city, and water, displays a subtle wealth of colours seldom found in Berlin's greyish contours. For anyone who spent their childhood in Berlin, no sunrise over the mountains or sunset at the lake can outshine the sweet dawns and dusks over the canal's spring and autumn foliage.

After the Herkules Bridge is a pedestrian bridge that arches like the ones in Chinese tableaus (and which, oddly, is called the Lützow Bridge, but it's named after the town, not the war hero). Between the two bridges is a sandy path up to the tiny park next to the sports clubhouse on Von-der-Heydt-Straße. It's mostly rear-courtyard buildings that line this riverside path; just a few entryways make this enchanted area a street with addresses. They seem to be portals to delight. Chestnut trees throw shadows on the ever-duskier path, and farther down the shore are the chestnut trees that the children of the Berlin west got to know in all seasons; their first and most pleasant botany lesson was the damp abundance of their buds, their flowers like tapers, and the brown fruits loosening themselves from thorny shells. In front of the little park, where the canal widens into a sort of duck pond, saplings lean over the water. As children, we asked their name and heard the words *weeping willow* for the first

---

1   Hessel is referring to Rosa Luxemburg.

time. From Königin-Augusta-Straße[2] on the northern bank of the canal, all side streets lead into the Tiergarten. The buildings here have held on to the good old days, with their columns and friezes and smooth espaliered walls. Here and there are a few mild lapses into the gothic or northern opulence, but they just end up looking peculiar, like artificial ruins in a well-made garden. The narrower the streets become, the more agreeable they are; for example, Hildebrandstraße or Regentenstraße.

One of them widens into a small square around the Church of St. Matthew; this narrow house of God, with a pointed tower and turrets, is built of the yellow and reddish brick that lends so many Berlin churches a similarity to Berlin train stations. It rises from tendrils of ivy, over lilac scrub, and it preserves some of the meagre nobility from the time when it was a meeting place for the pious upper crust, the lieutenants and privy councillors' daughters who prayed and danced together. The people called it the 'polka church'.

The pleasantly discreet character of Königin Augustastraße is disrupted in a few places by pretentious public buildings — Reichswehr ministries and social insurance offices and that sort of thing — but it still makes for a pleasant promenade along the river. The same is true of Schöneberger Ufer on the other side, where new constructions and renovations generally flow smoothly into the still waters of the older houses. Until recently, there was a small synagogue, with a low Arabian-style wall that we loved, just before the Potsdamerstraße intersection. It and its neighbours have now been swept away to make room for a new

---

2   Today known as Reichpietschufer.

building on the corner, similar to the ones rising on the other corners of the Potsdamer double bridge. There, our calm waters momentarily brush against a bit of densely populated big-city. At night, the rays of illuminated advertisements fall across it, and during the day, it's jolted by the thronging, faltering traffic. The four bronze gentlemen at the outer corners of both bridges aren't at all bothered by the urban noise, sitting with the tools of their trades on their pedestals. Each one has a naked little boy at his feet who is allowed to play with their sophisticated devices. Gauß and Siemens work diligently on their inventions and experiments without looking up, while Röntgen, who is actually wearing shoes with laces, shows his little one what he has made. And Helmholtz, the theorist, idly daydreams away. People of taste claim that the monuments aren't particularly well made, and the Baedeker agrees with them. I think they're rather harmless. There's something comforting about their presence, since one must often hazard to cross the roadway and enter their safe harbour. It's also nice that the gentlemen, all lightly clad in the same jackets, don't give a whit for the inclemency of the weather, and neither do their naked little boys.

We'll leave the Schöneberger Ufer behind us for a while and enter the corner building on Potsdamerstraße. Its exterior is decorated only with simple modern stripes painted in a yellow wash. But inside, plaster ornaments in the stairwell and on the various floors hark back to the days when it was a residential building for the haut bourgeoisie. Now the whole thing is an office building. Corporations make their homes here, with shortened names like Hibado and Raweci. There are lawyers' offices, and doctors' consultation rooms, and a big publishing house.[3] Since we're on friendly terms with the latter, we're allowed to enter its rooms and look out the window at the gingerbread cobbles of Am Karlesbad, an old side street that lags behind the times with its unkempt front gardens and once-stately crumbling balconies. Over there, nearly at Flottwellstraße, I know of a gateway where rails lead into a factory building in a courtyard. In that same courtyard, across from the modern factory, is a garden pavilion, perhaps the remainder of a country house on the old Potsdamer Chaussee, a tiny bourgeois Petit Trianon. A few happy steps lead up to a vine-covered forecourt with stone vases over the balustrade. From the glass veranda, instead of seeing a garden, you now look onto the custodian's chicken run and the overgrown wall of the neighbouring building. The prince of Prussia may have fled to a similar structure during the March Revolution of 1848, when he escaped through the Potsdamer Gate at dusk. Here, he could remain concealed in the old Karlsbad bathhouse. We hear a barrel organ accompanied by a voice, and we cross the hall to the windows over the courtyard. The yard lies in shadows below us, as with thousands of Berlin office buildings. Nothing but curtainless windows, and, behind them, the silhouettes of typewriters, shelves, and card indexes. But a few of the windows are open, and girls wearing black protective shirtsleeves look down at the music.

Once the canal passes the Potsdamer Bridge, it flows along tranquil shores for a while. Then viaducts overshadow it, it grazes the entryways of train stations, and finally it broadens

---

3   Hessel is referring to Rowohlt Verlag, where he worked as an editor.

into a rectangular harbour,[4] bordered by the offices of the railway. From time immemorial, a line of beautiful sycamores has stood along the harbour. If you'd like to travel from west Berlin to southern Europe, just pass by these trees on your way to Anhalter Station. Their brightly mottled trunks and shimmering greenery will remind you of eucalyptus trunks and olive leaves.

It's a short walk down the road to the elevated Gleisdreieck Station, a massive iron spider's web of tracks where freight trains, long-distance trains, and the subway converge, bucking forward on steam power or gliding electrically. Baedeker recommends going up there as part of a tour of the city, circle line, and elevated trains; the tour follows a new imaginary city wall built around old Berlin, and parts of earlier walls.

But now we're following the course of the canal, which traces a gentle curve next to the elevated train viaduct before separating from it at Hallesches Tor. Round crenelated towers rise in the picture: the gasworks, the oldest in Berlin, established in the 1820s by the English Imperial Continental Gas Association. Planufer stretches across the way. In the olden days, it was a suburban residential area, and it's still comfortable and spacious for walking. It leads past streets and squares whose names preserve the past: Am Johannestisch, Johanniterstraße, and Tempelherrenstraße.[5] A more recent, peculiar strand of history is located here: the City Mission, a creation of the famed court

---

4   Schöneberg Harbour was filled in in 1960. It is now the site of Mendelssohn-Bartholdy Park.

5   These names reference the Order of Saint John and the Knights Templar.

chaplain Stöcker. At its 'bread-roll church', beggars and the homeless receive two rolls, a cup of coffee, and a word for the soul; an auditorium in this Mission was once home to a burlesque theatre directed by Carli Callenbach.

Urbanhafen: a side arm of the canal flows around a trapezoidal island where boats are loaded and unloaded, and lift-bridges and cranes toil. But to the north, beyond the water, there is a battlefield of razing and construction — a city of ruins and a city coming into being. The whole area that was once the banks of the Luisenstadt Canal, from Engelbecken to the erstwhile pool at Wassertorplatz, has been drained to make room for a broad avenue that is being built from north to south.[6] Attracted by the chaos of sand and rubble, we walk toward Kottbusser Tor. There's construction on the elevated tracks at the moment, and we end up under a lurid minium-red network of iron girders. Kottbusserstraße leads us back to the canal, and we arrive at the bustling stalls of a market that stretches the whole length of Maybachufer. All of Neukölln seems to have come up from the south to shop. Everything is here: slippers and red cabbage, goat tallow and shoelaces, neckties and oil-packed herring. An old Jewess is spreading tattered furs and unpacking silks, and her neighbour eats a raw carrot in front of her vegetable cart. Across from the crude stink of fish, bottles of lily-of-the-valley fragrance promise a cheap, sweet scent. The other goods are interrupted by 'batches' of stockings made of silk gauze or indestructible 'armour silk'. Here and there, the shops lining the street spill

---

6   The Luisenstadt Canal connected the Spree at what is now Schillingbrücke to the Landwehr Canal at Urbanhafen. It was filled in in 1926.

out into the market. An enamel business sets up its wares right across the roadway. 'Tulip bulbs especially cheap before closing', 'Bargain sale, young lady', 'Real *biére blanche*', cries the market. 'Winter reds, all floury', one man extols of his potatoes. Next to him, there is something to see indeed, something that looks to us like it belongs in a museum collection: real hairpins, the long ones from our childhoods; and the round combs that women used to stick in their hair back then.

The mouth of the Neukölln Ship Canal, and the right angle it forms with the canal that is our current subject, is boarded up with all sorts of panels and board fences. As is so often the case, you can read the life of the city from its signs: 'Scaffold construction and rental business', 'Dogs clipped and docked', 'Pipes, beams, custom forms, fenceposts, scrap metal of all kinds', 'Altes Studentenbad bathing'. Black-and-white pennants flutter over these writings. But whatever they may have advertised is no more to be found.

Our canal divides itself again and enters the Spree as two arms. We walk along Freiarchengraben[7] and the rather meagre green of Schlesischer Busch Park, up to the river, which forms the broad bay of Osthafen at this point. A proud new stone ship with a red deck sets sail from the south: the new building of the Berlin Public Omnibus Corporation.

That's the Landwehr Canal. They say it's also going to be drained soon, that it isn't worth its keep anymore.[8] Then another piece of our lives would fade to a pale memory.

---

7 Freiarchengraben is called Flutgraben today.
8 The Landwehr Canal was never drained, of course.

Kreuzberg

It's obligatory. A landmark. The highest elevation above Spree-level. Since I haven't visited it for a while now, I decided to conscientiously observe it, and so I set out toward the south. On the way, on a side street of Großbeerenstraße, there were a few display windows where I had to pause for a minute. Kreuzberg could wait for me. One window guaranteed tailored textiles of all kinds, using their fabric or mine. Next to a row of lace pocket kerchiefs draped over a cord, a contemplative cloth doll leaned on her marble-grey arms. She had a red cap atop her blue-grey curls, an old colour, like those seen in ancestral portraits. It was hard to walk past her inviting eyes and arms. A few steps further, there was a bird and bird-feed store. It also had a few things for fish and against insects, and I read words like Piscidin, Wawil, Dermingin, Radicalin, and Milbin.[1] But it was a few lines of verse, rather pedestrian in content, that stayed in my memory:

> A little bird in your abode
> will be a joy to young and old.
> Large selection of song
> and domestic birds.

---

1   Pet-care product names.

I actually don't know if those last two lines are meant to be verse, but that's the way I read them.

All of that delayed me, understandably, but finally I stood in front of the waterfall at the foot of the hill in Viktoriapark. A faun-like bronze fisherman smiled at me from the water, wrangling a thrashing water sprite in his net. Besides me, a gigantic billboard girl stared at him in astonishment from the firewall on Kreuzbergstraße, without neglecting her work in any way. She applied highly recommended soap flakes to the laundry in her big tub. I followed a little boy heading uphill on his tricycle toward the sandbox. On the coast, whether in Ostend or the Riviera, people are said to lead a highly convivial beach lifestyle; in Berlin, there are various public parks, but also very nice sandboxes. Generally, they have a wooden rim where the little ones turn out their cake moulds, while inside, the bigger ones build mountains with tunnels and smoke holes for volcanoes on the broad sandy desert. Jealous and grown-up, I watch the busy bees playing within it and have a seat on a bench next to a couple of old women, whose conversation I catch only as a refrain, like a snippet of piano music prolonged by the pedal: 'An' then she went an' … now she's sure to … she had it all …' But I have more park and hill to see, and I dutifully seek out the monuments to the poets of the Napoleonic Wars, which are spread about in the greenery. Pleasantly enough, they're just herms,[2] harmless under the bushes and above the beds, like the ones who versify in Paris's Luxembourg Garden.

---

2   A herm is a type of portrait sculpture with a head and partial upper body on a quadratic pillar, sometimes with genitals.

Here, we have Friedrich Rückert with long hair and a bow tie. In a notebook broad enough to compose ghazals in, he works on a stanza whose level of complication inscribes lines into his forehead. Below, on his pedestal, a *bambino* plays a lyre. Not far away, Theodor Körner's collar rises to meet his sideburns, his head craning upward and to the left. His military coat is draped into a toga, and along with a scroll of poetry, he also holds a sword. Over there, Heinrich von Kleist isn't just holding his literary work in his left hand, he's also clutching his draped garment, while his right hand rubs a goose quill across his pensive chin. 'The Old Law' is written on Ludwig Uhland's scroll. He looks straight ahead with conviction. Pretty little blue flowers bloom in a bed in front of his pedestal. And there are more of them, blooming even more densely by the stream that branches from the waterfall. I walk up along it, thankful for everything that delays me on my way. There are still a few zoological and botanical distractions. Golden pheasants and deer behind a wire fence. You're allowed neither to tease nor feed them, the sign says — that would jeopardise the health and survival of the animal.

In front of the flowerbeds, which have informative porcelain labels, I hear voices next to me in conflict: 'All's I'm sayin' is that it's a rhoderdendra too, just another kind. It's written clear as day: "oriental".' By the peonies, a pale redhead asks me, 'Sir, could you tell me the time?' which admonishes me to hasten. So I don't stop in front of the sample portraits that the photographer is setting out halfway up the mountain, near the bridge over the waterfall.

And I don't stop at the low-lying milk spa,[3] where I could get a taste of a summer health resort. No, instead of recuperating, I climb the granite steps next to the artificial cliffs, sixty steps from the upper terrace to the big monument.

Next to me, a family man explains to his wife and children about all of the towers and roofs to be seen down there. He points out Anhalter Station, the dome of the Reichstag and the Victory Column, the nearby Church of Mercy and the far-off Luther Church. When he gets to the green patina-ed cupolas on Gendarmenmarkt, to St. Hedwig's Cathedral, the Berlin Cathedral, and the palace, his young daughter becomes impatient and asks, 'Why don't we go over by the little river?' By which she means the waterfall. Her father, however, manages to arrive at the churches of the old city. As he says their names, I think of who else might have looked down across the old towers over the course of history. Which reminds me of an anecdote about Prince Joachim, who spent a few strange hours up here consumed by fear and anxiety. His erudite astrologer Carion, for whom he constructed an observatory in his permanent residence at the Cölln Palace on the Spree, prophesied that on 15 July, 1525, a terrible storm would drown out the towns of Berlin and Cölln. As the chroniclers tell us, the day broke cloudless and at midday a blistering heat prevailed. The sky turned a wan yellow-grey, and, on the horizon, a black cloud appeared. There was unrest in the palace, the court carriages

---

3   Milk was often served as a health-improving drink at spas, similar to mineral water. Viktoriapark actually had its own dairy for the purpose, but the practice was losing popularity at the time Hessel wrote this.

were hastily hitched, and the prince dashed about his chambers, his expression haggard. As the wall of clouds towered higher and the first flashes of lightning trembled in the sky, the palace gates burst open and the prince, his wife, and their children drove in a four-in-hand coach across the palace square. The most highbred of the court, officers, and palace servants followed on horses and on foot, loaded with their swiftly bundled belongings.

The procession moved toward the south and the hills of the Cölln vineyards. Indeed, long ago there were vineyards here where wine really was cultivated. It's said to have been very sour, and yet it wasn't only drunk in Brandenburg, but also exported to Poland, Russia, and Sweden. Back then, spirits were a remedy for sore throats, gout, headaches, worms, and bad breath that could only be bought in pharmacies; after they became a popular drink, they supplanted wine production on the hills of Tempelhof. On the highest of those hills, which today is called Kreuzberg, the prince's procession sought shelter from the impending deluge. Up here, they waited for the storm that never came.

> But when he had tarried long atop and nothing came to pass, his wife (being a very Christian and god-fearing *Fürstin*) asked of him if he would not be pleased to return and persevere among his poor subjects ... He allowed himself to be influenced thus and at four in the afternoon he withdrew again to Cölln. But ere he arrived at the palace, a storm evidenced itself, and as he came to the palace gate, it smote the four horses and driver from before the princely carriage, but otherwise did no injury.

That is to be read in Peter Haffitz's *Mikrologikon*.[4]

What did the fearful monarch see when he gazed up at the menacing cloud and then down to his residence? Beyond the swamp and sand, a crenelated wall with turrets, behind it his fortress 'Castle Cölln' as the people called it, of which only its 'Green Cap' remains, that round tower on the Spree side with the green-patina-ed copper roof; the more distant domes and points of the clock towers of St. Peter's and the nearby Dominican cloister where Johann Tetzel had resided only a few years prior, in order to demonstrate the torments of hell to the Cöllners and Berliners, and to sell them indulgences ... And his gaze wandered further, over the House of the Holy Spirit[5] at St. Mary's and St. Nicolas's Church to the home of the Grey Brothers, and over the mills on the water. Then he looked upon Köpenick Gate, which he rode through to go hunting on that dark day when conspiring noblemen waylaid him on the heath. Joachim had the head of the boldest rebel displayed on a pike at the gate, and for an entire year it grinned down from its iron stake.[6] Between the churches and dignified corner buildings on

---

4   Various sources give 'Hafftitz's' name as Hafft or Hafftitius, and the name of the 1600 work as *Microcronicon* or *Microchronicon Marchicum*, [Chronicle of the Margraviate of Brandenburg].

5   A hospital located next to St. Mary's Church in medieval Berlin-Cölln.

6   No corroboration could be found for this story, though perhaps Hessel is confusing it with a similar one: while on a hunting trip together with the prince, the Junker von Otterstädt wrote a threatening message on Joachim's bedroom door to protest the execution of Junkers who were involved in highway robbery. Joachim had him drawn and quartered for high treason. See: George, Richard. *Hie gut Brandenburg alleweg! Geschichts- und Kulturbilder aus der Vergangenheit der Mark und aus Alt-Berlin bis zum Tode des Großen Kurfürsten.* Berlin: Verlag von W. Paulis Nachf. Jerosch & Dünnhaupt, 1900, p. 293.

Breiten Straße and Klosterstraße, only low thatched roofs and a few mossy tiled ones were to be seen, and much open field, tillage, and meadow, as well as ponds in the middle of the city.

From this hill, Swedes and the forces of the Kaiser alternately looked down on the embattled city during the Thirty Years' War, which the Great Prince[7] then briskly transformed into a walled fortress of cannons. In the Seven Years' War, the Austrians and Russians were here. They shot fiery cannonballs trailing long coronas of pitch and sulphur. Then our poor sand heap had a little bit of peace from world history. It wasn't until 1813 that the Berliners built defensive sconces on Tempelhof Hill and the Rollberge range.[8] But the enemy didn't reach the city — only the thunder of cannons from Großbeeren was to be heard. Soon after, bells rang in thanks for the victory at Leipzig.

In 1818, the cornerstone was laid for the victory monument towering here behind me. The sovereigns of Russia and Prussia threw lime from a trowel onto the stone's bed. And then Schinkel's monument sprang up, completely cast in iron in the so-called 'old-German style,' as a contemporary reported, 'on an octagonal foundation that formed a raised stone-tiled terrace around the monument, rising up on eleven octagonal steps ... In whole and in part, the architecture of the Cologne cathedral served as a model ... The aggregate forms a tower-like baldachin over twelve alcoves or niches, which form the cross-shaped basis for the entirety. These niche-like alcoves are dedicated to the twelve major battles of the great war and

---

7   Friedrich Wilhelm I.
8   During the course of the Napoleonic Wars.

each niche is occupied by symbolic figures of victory that correspond to various events. The pleasant task of sculpting these figures has been fortuitously accomplished by Professors Rauch, Tieck, and Wichmann ...'

Made dizzy by the thoughts of days gone by, as well as by the evening breeze that carries the scent of malt over from the breweries, just like in Munich, I would have liked to ask someone: where is the little ravine the people once called the Gloomy Cellar? It must have once been here on the slope. In prehistoric times, it was a ravine where burial urns with ashes were placed. Then in Old Fritz's days, a curious hermit made his home there.[9] Then it was a popular day-trip destination. And in the secretive days before liberation from Napoleon, the patriotic gymnasts Jahn and Friesen formed the secret society of the Deutscher Bund here, together with their friends, to fight for freedom from the French. But then, suddenly, in the east I see a plane over Tempelhof and I'm called back to the present.

---

9   Legend has it that while walking past the ravine in 1740, King Friedrich
    Wilhelm I asked the hermit who resided there to present himself. When
    the hermit claimed to have once read aloud from the Psalms to the king's
    grandfather, Friedrich Wilhelm offered him a golden coin, to which the hermit
    replied, 'That coin is too big for me, I take only copper.'

Tempelhof

Yes, right over there is our big airport. You can watch the buzzing steel birds glide down onto green expanses and roll onto the tarred runways. They ascend again, circle, and fly off in all directions. In Lufthansa's hangars, they stand next to each other like locomotives in their sheds. The crowd casts a connoisseur's eye on all this coming and going. The smallest boys speak about airfoils and wingspan in the tones of confident men. In fact, they were out there at the 'ILA', the Berlin Air Show. They know all about soaring aircraft, monoplanes and biplanes, just as they know all of the car models — just start a conversation with them in front of the exhibition halls and you'll see. Often what they say is utter nonsense, the real experts have assured me, but these tiny Berliners present it with such marvellous dryness and certainty. It's also strange how ungrudgingly even the poorest little ones look at all of this equipment. A communal or communicable joy must be contained in the whirring of the propeller and the rolling of the planes across the tarmac, in the incessant sound of exploding petrol. If you can't afford a car, become a chauffeur. Or maybe fly a plane, think some of the little ones, when they see the pilots walk by in their creaking leather suits, their curious batwing uniforms.

Athletic fields begin where the airport ends, and the boys

run over to their soccer teammates. This large territory belongs to the children and the aeroplanes. And yet it wasn't so long ago that it was the site of old-fashioned parades and military reviews. The very opposite of athletic elasticity prevailed here: the rigid goose-step of the guard. Twice a year, the units from the Berlin garrisons were trotted out by their highest commanders. From the days of Friedrich the Great up to the World War, this is where the final assembly took place before entering the campaign. Hopefully, that sort of thing won't happen again for a long time on these sorriest of all fields, which are as sobering as the barracks that sometimes filled them. Instead of barracks, residential developments have been established here, like New Tempelhof just around the corner, with its quiet rings of green space, pretty garden gateways, and streets that rise and fall toward buildings that remind me of old Potsdam.

There isn't much of the original village left in Tempelhof, which is named after the Knights of Templar. Even the little granite church in the parish park takes a different form now. There's nothing from the village except a few sunken one-storey houses with front yards, which are also found here and there in Berlin suburbs. The Tempelhof of today is one of hideous, hurried construction from the time after 1870, built entirely according to the tastes of the construction companies and contractors. Such buildings are scattered all too frequently around Berlin's outskirts, and only now are they being supplanted by new housing blocks without side or back buildings, without 'Berliner Zimmer' or moulding on their facades.

But there are two monuments to our new era — the Ullstein Printing Press with its proud sixteen-storey tower, and the Sarotti factory building, both on the Teltow Canal. In the former, the result of the editorial and typesetting acumen collected at the publisher's building on Kochstraße is sent on its way through all kinds of rotary presses, high-speed printing machines, folding, binding, and collating machines in order to become magazines, newspapers, booklets, and books. In the other, cacao beans travel far from the tropics to pass through brush rollers, crushing, shelling, cleaning, and moulding machines, becoming lovely packaged chocolate. It's astounding how our hazy writings and ideas grow into endless, neatly printed masses of paper, and how dust-covered, wrinkly sacks of compressed beans become countless immaculate bars and truffles. It's all carried out by cleverly devised wheels and rollers, which rotate, stamp, grab, and spin. We ignorant visitors stand quietly while their thousand custodians in smocks and caps, both men and women, smile at our astonished faces. (These past days I have met a veritable army of tranquil Berlin working women, unfortunately only in passing. I would like to be there, invisible, when they sit together in the cafeteria, and hear what they say to each other on their way home, what they think about life ...)

Yes, we stand there stunned in the gigantic hall and look up at the rolls of paper coming down from the ceiling, lowering themselves into the ironclad devices that grasp and turn them, emerging as separate, finished, illustrated magazines. We creep through the hall of 'long conches', where a roller moves over the grinding trough, granite on granite, pushing along the mass of chocolate, which then flows into bar moulds, filling machines, and conveyor belts. Without ever being touched by a human hand, the chocolate slips into tinfoil, wax, and parchment paper; into box and carton.

Next to Tempelhof is Mariendorf, where I would never have gone if one of those talented and happy women who work with the flickering silver screen hadn't taken me into the glass building where films are shot. All around are barren outskirts and boondocks. But inside is a fantastic living world. Are those barracks or backdrop, a bivouac or nursery there in the alternating darkness and light? A few uneven steps lead down into an alpine landscape, before which a health spa, train station, and enchanting little train are set up like playthings. Around the next corner, you see a life-size model of some train cars. We're allowed to climb around in it, into the sleeper car where an abandoned bride will awaken to her horror. We stand in the aisle, looking at the doors and windows, bedsteads and ceiling, all of the authentic details. And next to us stands the very same delicate beauty who moments ago was lying there in the lamplight. Then she leads us over to the berth where filming is currently underway. We stand behind the man in charge of the spotlight. Next to him is a director giving cues. The man at the piano plays a dance melody. And now the people at the bar begin to move in the harsh light. It's a sort of *Karneval* celebration. Confetti streamers are thrown across dress coats and bare shoulders. Wild masked faces besiege the couples dancing on the dais. One man sits alone with his glass, elbows propped on the bar in the middle of the revellers, staring and withdrawn. Someone whispers a famous name to us. Now he raises his head and looks over at us. 'He's looking at us as if we were ghosts,' I say. 'No,' I'm informed, 'he can't see anything but a blinding light!' The music switches off. The director goes over to the bar patrons, debriefing them on their performance. Then these patient souls must revel once again, and, in their midst, the man must stare again. 'It's a tiring trade,' says our guide, She Who Would Know. 'And the worst bits are all the waiting and always having to be ready. It's like being in the military.' Of course, we laypeople are eager to join, even if it were just as extras. We would like to appear on the screen, to see ourselves acting just once.

Berliners are passionate cinema-goers. The newsreel provides us with all of the world history we've missed out on this week. The most beautiful women of both continents are ours every day, smiling and crying in the moving pictures. We have our great picture-palaces around the Memorial Church on Kurfürstendamm, near Potsdamer Platz, in the suburbs, as well as the thousand small cinemas whose bright, enticing lights can be seen on dim streets in every district. Oh, and there are even a bevy of matinee cinemas, proper warming shelters for the body and soul. At the cinema, the Berliner isn't as critical, or at least not as dependent on newspaper critics as he is at the theatre. He lets himself be overwhelmed by the illusion. It is life by proxy for the millions who would like to forget their monotonous routine. There is no pause to the awakenings and reveries. Nowhere can you experience popular longings and collective pleasures like in the '*Kientopp*', where the only musical accompaniment is a mournful piano. But sometimes, when our tears fall uncontrollably to some stirring scene, I think I would prefer to hear the barrel-organ music that once roared, then whispered, in our courtyards.

Hasenheide

'Hasenheide' means 'rabbit heath', but there aren't rabbits here anymore, and no heath either. But if you're interested in the names of different parts of the city and their original meanings, you might like to know that in 1586, according to the chronicles of the Cölln town clerk, a princely decree was enacted: 'On this 18th of May, the citizens are both enjoined by his princely grace to follow his solemn command to make holes in garden fences, that hares may enter.' Later, Friedrich Wilhelm I responded to an appeal for pasturing rights on the heath: 'It shall remain a garden for rabbits.' Under Friedrich the Great, the first country inns were established, and after the Napoleonic Wars came garden coffeehouses. Between them lay a gigantic fairground stretching from Bärwaldstraße to the athletic fields, with dice stalls, strength tests, muscular maidens, tightrope walkers, and marvellous animals. In front of the dance hall, a cigar seller walked back and forth with his wooden box slung around his neck — for here, the tobacco forbidden elsewhere could be smoked — offering fatwood and tinder and crying, *'Cigaro avec du feu.'*

The beer and coffee gardens remain to this day, and have continually expanded. They're almost *too* big. They reflect the monstrosity of our era of giant portions and double concerts.

They try to outdo each other: 'Enthralling concert on the terrace every day, free entry', one entryway thunders at us, and not far from there, an establishment is and will remain 'the leading cafe, despite all of the new openings'. It promises 'daily dancing on an illuminated glass floor', with music by a certain 'Rheingold Band'. But the old fairgrounds aren't there any longer. Today, the 'Neue Welt' is one of the biggest garden establishments, with halls for meetings and celebrations. Older people will remember the days when the words 'Neue Welt' brought to mind panoramas, museums of science, 'savages', female animal-trainers in riding boots, and muscle men. As a small child, I saw the smiling mouth and rosy cheeks of a girl whose head was cut off and set on her body again, as well as what was perhaps the first woman without a torso, who made beautiful motions with her arms while the magician recited Heine's verses about the lotus flower that fears the sun; and surely it was here that I heard the name Dante for the first time, in a shack where the torments of his hell were sculpted panoramically. Very gruesome. Nothing like that is on offer these days.

Another piece of Hasenheide remains: even if it's only as a bust, the founder of the German gymnastics movement, Friedrich Ludwig Jahn, still looks down upon athletic youths, not far from where the very first gymnastics team met. Jahn looks complacently at the tan boys and girls in swimsuits kicking and hurling their balls, here as on so many other squares in Berlin. In the old garden, where families can make coffee, there are some dramatic pieces of rubbish from an abandoned shooting range that look almost like ruins. In the middle of the targets, you can still make out faded silhouettes of the enemy. We are living in an age that requires such props to convince us that people were once foolish enough to shoot at each other with guns. A photographer's advertisement set up near the entrance to the street seems downright old-fashioned. It depicts the prize-winning models from a hairdressing contest in Neukölln. We gaze on the complicated undulations of lush tresses, as they are never to be seen anymore in the wild, not even in the most secluded hinterlands of Neukölln.

Through Neukölln Toward Britz

There's really no reason to visit Neukölln for its own sake. Maybe beautiful new architecture will appear one day behind the gigantic scaffolding that currently towers over Hermannplatz, roughly where the district begins. But the true Neukölln consists of those suburbs that had hardly ten thousand residents in the 1870s but now have between two and three hundred thousand. Of course, a bronze Kaiser Wilhelm I rides on horseback on Hohenzollernplatz. The broad streets house many emporiums, cinemas, taverns, steamed-sausage stalls, radio hobby shops, and stately facades that conceal the misery of the courtyard apartments. Between Hermannstraße and Bergstraße, there's also an area where the squalor is more visible, known as Bullenviertel, where work-weary people pour out of overfilled trams in the evening, and myriad sickly children roam about on the street. A desolate district. When it was still a day-trip destination called Rixdorf, it may have been more interesting. I have scant knowledge of this suburb — I've never been able to convince myself to visit its newer monuments, the fountain dedicated to Fritz Reuter and the statue of Friedrich Wilhelm I (who founded a settlement of pious Bohemians here). I've always just ridden the tram through Neukölln to get elsewhere. Mainly Britz. If you pass a few dear little summer cottages from the old days, and the gas station with its Olex and Shell signs, and then turn into the centre of this little suburb, you'll find yourself on a winding road that leads down to a wooded hillside. Cross the path bordered with 'broken-down fencing', and behind trees and ponds — a happy sight — the settlement appears.[1] Its colours flash yellow, white, and red, interspersed with blue borders and balcony walls. We walk down one of the streets radiating from the round complex, along the open side of a rectangle. Its three other sides are lined with narrow apartment buildings around a large garden plot. There are no back buildings to be found. The stairwells are housed in round protuberances. Everyone has his little plot of garden, just like in the clusters of summerhouses, only better tended and within a much more communal whole.

We've arrived at the inner ring and we finally see the pond, the centre whose sloping banks are ringed by the horseshoe-shaped building. Skylights, windows large and small, and colourful recessed balconies lend the homes an appealing symmetry. On the side where the horseshoe tapers, this happy little city has its marketplace: consumer cooperatives, which provide the settlement dwellers with foodstuffs in a socially sensible manner, I'm assured. We enter one of the homes. It's also colourful inside, but without any superfluous embellishments, everything unadorned and yet adorned. This settlement represents the boldest foray into the limbo between city and country. Here, as in Lichtenberg, Zehlendorf, and the

---

1   Here, Hessel describes Bruno Taut's celebrated *Hufeisensiedlung* ('Horseshoe Estate'). A landmark of modernism and urban housing, it was named a UNESCO World Heritage Site in 2008.

other ends of the city, many factors were at work to create humane habitations: a housing shortage; a longing for all that is beautiful; the centering of life around the communal; and the zeal of this new generation of architects. Their work is constantly advancing, and it is the most important thing happening to Berlin now. I can't yet describe this new emerging Berlin — I can only praise it.

Steamship Music

'Bricks can be taken free of charge. Inquire with the foreman.'
Those are the bricks of the old bridge, Jannowitz Bridge, that's
being demolished because many new things are being built
right in the middle of the old harbour city of Cölln am Wasser.
The subway is being re-tunnelled. Hissing and pounding noises
envelop the steel scaffolding and barrels. I wend my way past
rubble and barricades to the landing for steamships heading
up the Spree. Pleasure steamers with music. That's something
I'd like to experience; it's even in the Baedeker — which
I'm always studying so eagerly — under 'Day 4, Afternoon:
Steamship Ride to Grünau'. But instead of Grünau, the man
at the steamship company's counter wants me to go to the
Woltersdorf lock. I have no idea why. He's stern with me,
like many of his ilk in Berlin. He allows me to eat first, in the
restaurant on the water. Meanwhile, the steamship fills up and
the best seats are taken. I consider taking the next one, which
leaves a half hour later, but at the decisive moment I'm ordered
onto the first one and shipped off. Once again, I find myself
settling into old-fashioned surroundings. Indeed, there are
people sitting here who are still fat. The slim, athletic youth
of today speeds past us in racy motorboats; we sit here like in
old Berlin caricatures — portly gentlemen in their golden years

and madams in voluminous mountains of fabric. We move forward at a painful crawl, idle and redundant between all of the industrious iron-framed warehouses, bricks, and cranes on the banks.

There are wheat mills with gigantic elevators that lift the grain from barges, and others that suck it out with exhaust fans. It enters the mill, where it's weighed, sieved, washed, dried, crushed, milled, sieved again, poured into sacks — all of this on a conveyor belt, in a uniform fashion — and returned to the barge as processed flour for further transport. We pass under the Oberbaum Bridge. I glance from its new old-Brandenburg-style watchtowers to the refrigerated warehouse towering over Osthafen, nearly complete behind its scaffolding. In vast storerooms, thousands upon thousands of eggs, and gigantic shipments of vegetables, fruit, and meat are stockpiled until they are needed. Over at the Treptow beach, green park meets the water. I'd like to get out and walk over to the children on the swing carousel. The miniature train must still be there, chugging round its track just like the ones that are assembled and wound up in childhood bedrooms. There were three open touring cars that circled the track twice behind a little cloud of smoke, with bells and whistles that rang out when you crossed the field and at both tunnels. 'Klettermaxe' was the name of the engine, where the conductor sat. The restuarant there is called Eierhäuschen, and the street behind it leads to the big astronomical observatory. There's also a large expanse of lawn where people can camp freely, like on the public lawns at Versailles. I'd like to get out, but our steamship doesn't stop. On our left, 'Gelsenkirchen on the Spree' appears: Oberschönweide,[1] and Rummelsburg behind it. On the shore, barges are being loaded with slag in front of the metal works. Behind it is the red textile factory, the transformer factory, and, far in the distance, the gigantic brick form of the Klingenberg power plant. All of this smoking, towering industriousness puts our luxurious inactivity and contemptible snail's pace to shame. Now we're even making music!

We pass Köpenick, which offers less temptation to disembark, though I know that the palace and chapel lie beyond the old moat that's now a duck pond. It's the palace where Prince Joachim lived with his Spandau beauty Anna Sydow, the palace where his archenemy, the knight von Otterstedt wrote the famed words on his door:

> Joachim, Joachim, be wary.
> We catch ye, we'll hang ye.

But to get there, you have to walk through the typical tedium of dismal housing blocks and squares named after Kaiser Wilhelm. Behind the palace, however, you'll find Wendenkietz, with its fishermen's shacks, fish traps, nets, and weathered stonework around the old marketplace ... but I find myself surrounded by motionless bodies that are completely devoted to steamship music and indolence. I can't get through. Young folks wave at us in pity from the many boathouses, bathing

---

1 Gelsenkirchen was an important industrial hub, and similarly, Oberschöneweide was home to much heavy industry.

facilities, and beaches. All around me, my shipmates wave back. Waving is the main occupation of those on a steamship.

Now we're being transported across the lake, and we stop at an inn, where we're supposed to eat enormous pork knuckles — that has been despotically decreed in writing. Since many people are getting off here, I'm not trapped on board all the way to the Woltersdorf lock; I climb down the steps leaning against the side. After giving up my return ticket, I hasten past the pork knuckles and into the forest, where I walk along sandy paths, under pines that take on Chinese silhouettes in the afternoon light.

When I reach the avenue, I'm in luck. A car appears and I recognise it: a friend's Graham-Paige. I wave like the shipwrecked. After so many plump neighbours on the steamship, I'm suddenly sitting next to the slimmest of young lady Berliners, a child's balloon from Treptow fluttering brightly behind her. We drive at an invigorating speed, past cottages huddled between fields of grain and gently sloping hills. Königs Wusterhausen is over there. The tower of the Telefunken station is an iron spider's web. We see the pretty yellow front building of the hunting chateau where the 'Tobacco Cabinet' had its meetings.[2] We are familiar with the table of this smoking brotherhood from the Hohenzollern Museum. I describe the king's court jester — a certain Professor Gundling — to my chauffeur. We chat about this poor fool and his world as we

---

2   Though not his invention, the 'Tabakskollegium' is closely associated with King Friedrich Wilhelm I, who held informal gatherings at which men of high social standing smoked tobacco and discussed politics in an informal setting.

travel down the long road toward Storkow. In half darkness, we drive forested routes toward Lake Scharmützel.

It's late, and we're sitting on the terrace of a hotel in Saarow. There's dancing going on up above us. By the water there are footlights that lift a bit of lake out of the night.

We'll stay here tonight, and tomorrow we'll see the broad lake from our windows. Then we'll drive out via Pieskow and stop at the pretty Meckerndorf actors' colony hidden in the greenery. And in Saarow itself we'll even visit one of the houses of a painters' colony with bold gables. Will we speed across the lake in a motorboat, into the far fingers of its shores? Or walk through the woods to the Markgrafen Boulders? Or take the paths that run closest to the water?

Too bad it's already too late in the year for a swim.

To the East

Is it still worth speaking of the Alexanderplatz of today and yesterday? It will already have disappeared by the time these lines are printed. The trams, buses, and crowds of people must already bypass the fenced construction sites and deep lacerations in the earth. The plump city goddess Berolina, who once regulated comings and goings from a tall pedestal here, has now wandered off. The lanes of the neighbouring Scheunenviertel — crooked and straight, infamous and wretchedly honest — are mostly demolished now. The walls of the police headquarters loom bleakly to the south over the piles of rubble. From the northeast, the high tower of St. George's Church soars above buildings and fences. Police station and church will remain as they are. As for whatever else is still standing here, almost all of it will be torn down or overhauled. Most parcels of land are already owned by the train and subway company, which is digging its tunnel to the east. However much of it they later cede, the new owners won't be allowed to build on it according to their discretion; all future construction here is determined by the blueprints of the municipal planning office. So there's no danger of speculators choking everything with piles of ugly tenement blocks and gloomy, airless side and rear buildings. A horseshoe of high-rise buildings is planned around a centre island with a roundabout.

In those places where the old is disappearing and the new is taking its place, a transitory world materialises, haphazard, agitated, impoverished in the ruins. If you know the nooks and crannies here, you can find peculiar lodgings, ghastly things somewhere between nests and caves. For example, one is hidden in the basement rooms of a big demolished tenement that once stored fruit for the nearby market hall. Behind the rubble and mortar of the 'banana cellar', there is a desolate bed for homeless people who no longer can or want to go to the night shelters. They crawl into their corners here when the bars all around Alexanderplatz close. When we unauthorised intruders stumble past them, they pull their legs up a little closer to their bellies, and tug their jackets down over their knees. Other basement rooms contain little bazaars whose contents remind me of Parisian flea markets: jam jars, carbide lamps, birdcages, wastepaper baskets, old top hats, chimneys for oil lamps, Russian tunics, shoes 'hardly worn', shoelaces, oil paintings with 'gold' frames, eiderdowns, and even ostrich feathers. The world above is also full of street trade. At the entrance to the St. George's Church square, prostitutes sneak around the corner in the freezing rain and then stop in their tracks. Through a hole in the fence surrounding the demolition, I saw a greyed old woman handing out durable white-linen undergarments to the poor creatures. They're supposed to put them on over their lace 'lingerie' to keep the cold out.

Walking past the ruins, which are reminiscent of the rubble

of a city that has been shot to bits, we arrive at Münzstraße to a
thronging crowd. A woman is lying on the ground in front of the
tavern. Hovering over her, still in a boxer's stance, is one of those
fellows in cap and sweater who are so prevalent around here.
Bystanders look on with interest. No one dares to intervene. No
'cop' shows his face either. The justice carried out here enjoys a
general acceptance. We're shoved on. 'Yer all just leftovers from
yesterdee,' someone shouts at our little group. On the next street
over — and I'm not sure if it was the one closer to or farther from
Alexanderplatz — people are milling around a street merchant.
There he is with neckties draped over his arm: 'Everything for a
mark. Everybody in showbiz wears my ties.' The man over there
with the shoelaces seems to be building to an eloquent crescendo,
but we can't push through the crowd around him. 'Trick matches,'
someone cries from the right, next to a stand with calling cards
that can be taken home straight from the embossing machine.
Warm steam rolls up the sign that reads: 'Horsemeat Bouletten,
5 ct.' Now I think we're on Neue Königstraße. The signs over the
stores interest me most: 'Canine Clinic and Grooming, Dog and
Horse Clipping Service', and in smaller type beneath it, 'Docking,
castrating, painless dstryng'. 'When it's a new hat, it has to be a
Cityhat'. 'Artists' Curtains'. (What could those be?) And in front
of a low-set door, 'Caution! Rat poison has been spread here in
the cellar'. One store contains two businesses: translation and
skilled fabric repair.

Back to the area around Alexanderplatz and to the east. Was
it on one of these corners, out on some walk or another ... or
did I only dream that I saw the word 'hotel' written backwards

and upside-down? A strangely macabre sight that made the entire house uncanny, this ꞀƎꞀOH!

For another long stretch, I barely look at the road and the people. My eyes are glued to the gigantic advertisements on board fences and display windows, at little shops and big closing sales. In a tobacco shop's display, a nymph in a loincloth kneels under a tree with stylised leaves. An ashtray with a stoneware cigarette lies next to her as if it were a jug. That's 'Flora Privat, light, sweet, aromatic, the victress among 2-pfennig cigarettes'. In the stationery and accessories store, there are songbooks about wine and Rhine, peculiar joke compendiums, and 'the new jingling bell bracelets for dancing, an enticing gift'. Some of the neologisms are surprising. I've seen 'Naturange' in other parts of the city as well, but the vermouth 'Stilla Sana' I've only seen here. It stands next to well-known high-quality wines as well as inexpensive ones 'with 5% rebate for confirmations and youth ceremonies'. Also astounding: 'Intestinal Lubricant Rodolax'. The largest ladies can find corsetry here, suitable for even the most robust figures; for example, the new hip shaper with stomach cinch. For the 'gentleman', there are dancing shoes with very pointy tips. A black strap binds the beetle-brown midsection of a walking shoe. Naive middle-class conventions abound: 'Credit is a double misfortune: goods and customer, both gone', one innkeeper had posted on the door of his brandy bar. A picture of a lion hangs over the electric piano in the Grüne Quelle, with the following beneath it: 'Roar like a lion roars when you need another pour'. Next to the orgy of advertising at Kitchen

Heaven and Cohn's Furniture, the faded lettering over a garden store seems touchingly quaint: 'Flowers for joy and sorrow'.

Our reading leads us to Große Frankfurterstraße. We're deafened by the sawing and rattling coming from behind the wooden fence that blocks off the middle of the avenue. A wax mannequin in a country-style dress and white bonnet smiles down on the men hammering and pulling winches. She's standing in the window of a store labelled 'Festival Wardrobe — for harvest festivals and children's parties, *Trachten* in folk and regional styles'. The iron scaffolding around the steam-powered pile-driver soars four stories high. Over there, where the cobbles are torn up, cement sacks shimmer springtime green on the autumn street. A worker empties them one after the other. He's also wearing a green jacket that is illuminated by the gas flame next to his machine, much like the greenery is lit up by candelabra-style streetlamps on more upscale avenues. He dumps the cement where other workers are shovelling a brown mass. The mixture goes into a container, which swivels like an excavator, pouring its moist contents into a waiting trolley. The trolley carts its prize to where the previous layer is already drying, and the wet layer is pasted over the dry one. Little boys stare open-mouthed at the spectacle. Grown-ups stop in their tracks too. Berliners still know how to gape at things, just like in the old days when they weren't in such a hurry. Their technical knowledge seems to have grown in the meantime, though. They aren't the naive folk that the painter Theodor Hosemann once caricatured staring at the great pipes of the English Gas Association, saying: 'If I could jes' figger out how they get the oil up there through these here cannons.'

More promising sites await us at the curb. The Hackebär Bar manufactures its own sausage. Their new folk ensemble is there. The old excitement will be back again, the atmosphere and humour. A crowd is already waiting under the fluttering pennants. A white cardboard barber and hairdresser are pasted to the wall of the entryway. They lure clients toward a salon in the back building. Massive movie posters announce the arrival of America's most famous cowboy, as well as the Count of Cagliostro. He sneers at a brunette furrowing her brow over a fan. Dark side streets with bland, old-fashioned names interrupt our garish path. Oh, the old wine cellar with its inviting welcome sign on the slanting wall above its steep staircase!

Now we're standing at the gateway to Rose-theater. 'The Spendthrift, a romantic folk play by Ferdinand Raimund' is on the program. It's not starting for another ten minutes. We still have time to walk down to the end of the entryway, and up to the autumnal skeleton of the pergola's foliage, which in summertime forms a canopy. A brick wall reaches to the sky — like the curtains before a theatre show begins — and before it stands a quaint, bright little house with green pilasters and window frames. Maybe the people who once owned the theatre lived here; back then the entrance must have been on the garden side, because a wide old terrace leads up into the theatre on this side.

We take our seats in the auditorium and look around a little. So many girls in pink and powder-blue blouses! And with bare arms, though not entirely bare like our deeply décolletéed women in west Berlin have them, but rather with a broad satin stole over the shoulders. Look down into the orchestra, in its low-set box as red as oxblood. Look up at the silvery swans nuzzling each other's throats under the balustrade.

The curtain rises, revealing a sumptuous hall belonging to the titular Spendthrift, who has many friends and lackeys. The colours of the walls and garments resemble those in our favourite children's books, and there are little sofas like in our sisters' doll parlours. The fairy Cheristane stands stiffly and gracefully; her backdrop is an entire magical world made up of cliffs and sky. She has a child's voice, the voice of an eager child reciting a text. She says her verses to the audience, not toward her beloved fosterling. His grieving gestures are also aimed at us. That makes it more poignant. She describes the apparitions in her mind's eye, and as she does so, they sweep past the back wall along the sky. Then she sinks below the stage.

It's a beautiful old theatre, where the beggars have wonderful monks' habits and wavering rods. Where flashes of sea-storm lightning blaze above a rocking ship, illuminating the clouds much more marvellously than the Berlin Week of Lights illuminates its monuments. Go to the east, quickly, as long as there is still such old red-gold theatre behind the cinemas and variety shows!

And yet, we've missed out on the many cinemas and variety shows in the area. We *could* still go to the Zur Möwe dance hall, where an old-fashioned German ball for mature youths is taking place. But a wave of Sunday evening theatre-goers pushes us in the opposite direction down Frankfurter Allee. A memory surfaces. January 1919: grenades were flying through the air here.[1] The battle of Lichtenberg! If you were pushed back into the narrow lanes, you'd find smugglers of jewels, soap, and English tobacco; men clad in field-grey selling smoking paraphernalia, and chocolate from the occupied zones; barrel organs playing The Marseillaise, plucked guitars …

A wobbling carriage jostles us back to Alexanderplatz and a few streets to the north. It stops in front of a raucous, overflowing tavern. The trumpet player has a frizzy head of hair and puffed cheeks, and music flows over the tumblers and beer glasses, the girls' Slavic cheekbones and the delicate insolence of the boyish faces. A woman with *broderie anglaise* on her collar accompanies him on the piano. The thick-necked owner forces us into a rather unfavourable position among his regular guests. They like to hear 'I Kiss Your Hand, Madame' just as much here as in the west, but then it's negated by a sort of military march that everyone sings along to with Prussian fervour. There's no reason to believe that we've stumbled into a nationalistic tavern, though. Soon, a lad comes by our table collecting money to support the people on strike in the west. He wants us to sign a petition. A sentimental song about the Rhine wafts up to a banner reading 'Giant steamed sausages 50 ct.' A few boys take a seat on one side of our table and shift slowly toward us, leery at first, then more cordially. Based on both the things they exaggerate and the things they understate, it's to be gathered that they don't have any 'digs'. They don't want to sleep at the friends' they happened to meet yesterday. Maybe they'll 'pound

---

1   Hessel is referring to the Spartacist uprising. It consisted of a general strike which was violently crushed by the Freikorps militia.

the ground' if they can't find anything else. In some buildings, you can find a sweet-natured resident who will bring a warm cup of morning coffee to those sleeping on the ground; maybe he himself slept under the railway viaduct in his youth. He knows how it is to have no place to hang your hat. One of the boys leads us on through a series of tasteless and gloomy dens. He knows a 'grand' place for dancing. It's called something like 'Polarstern', and it's a subterranean chamber with a stiff, dusty wooden lambrequin over the door to a side room. Pairs of girls and boys step forward to dance, accompanied by two musicians playing the piano and violin. They dance with fervour, as we are accustomed to seeing in similar clubs, and even more frantically, or at least it seems to us, and more hedonistically — as if misery or danger were lying in wait.

Our guide has to move on (and in this matter, we elegant idlers are in agreement), to Kommandantenstraße and then past Hallesches Tor. On the way, he wants to show us something by the market hall. Once again, we find ourselves across from the police headquarters. He pushes us through a low gate into the warming shelter. He tells us about the figures, some upright, others lying down. He differentiates between locals and those who are 'just passing through'. You're not allowed to smoke here, or sing, or play cards, or do any business. But a bit of business goes on anyway, mainly bartering, it would appear. The currency? Clothing that has been received as a gift or 'found', and which fits someone else better. A man close to the oven trades a pulp novel for some bread. Are those foot wraps or newspapers that the man is pulling out of his empty boots over there on the wooden bench? On my way out, I see that we're under the railway viaduct. We come to a street that smells of fruit, but the fruit warehouse looks like an office building. Even during the day, nothing is sold to individual customers here. Berlin's marketplaces don't spread out onto the street like those of Paris. There are quaint displays in the windows. One of them just has cardboard and packing paper: 'Butcher paper and waxed paper'. 'Paper sausage plates in all sizes and price ranges'. Scale pans, trays, and accessories. A cat guards an entire rustic cabin made of hemp. Around the corner there's a kosher restaurant, and a hotel whose curtains are secretively drawn. A sheet hangs on a windowless wall like election hoardings: 'Autumn's first German carp'.

We pass under the viaduct's iron columns. This urban railway architecture looks so old-fashioned today. Just a glimpse of a waiting room. Sleeping people lean against bundles and sacks. The empty glass and dull tin of an abandoned buffet. Outside, half-asleep horses stand with legs stiffly splayed in front of a waiting wagon. In a bar, market hands wait until it's time to go to work, and the unemployed wait for an opportunity. A few chauffeurs are stirring cups of broth. Market-hopping merchants show each other items from their baskets and discuss the 'situation' in mercantile terms. A man in shirtsleeves walks between the tables, keeping an eye on acquaintances and strangers alike. He is, according to our guide, the 'bouncer'. There's no work for him today, though. An old man is seated, babbling into his beard, along with a fat woman who has nodded off over her basket. A hand-written announcement hangs over them: 'Goose-gutting shop for rent for the season (good foot traffic)'. We're refused entry at a beer pub across the way. It's for travelling merchants only. They're the brokers between the small-time farmers and the Berlin vegetable shops.

Now it's time to enter the hall itself. Inside we're tolerated as tourists, but we aren't welcomed with the sympathetic irony that greets the *noceur* at the booths in Paris. Women gaze up querulously from the potatoes they're peeling. A boy standing next to his wagon in a velvet cap and nice bucket-top boots glowers in our direction, as does another one wearing a lustrous green jacket that gleams through the dimness. Only a short grey-headed man nods at us in a friendly fashion as he comes in through a dark side-entrance under the 'Resi is better than Rahma' advertisement, whispering obscenely about various brands of margarine in a Saxon accent. We stumble out between leeks, scallions, and turnips.

* * *

Home. A few hours of sleep. At six, I have a rendezvous at Berlin's other main hall, the flower market.

An early-morning moon over barren blue asphalt. Daytime and nighttime lights are reflected in the armour-like panelling of the elevated train station. A nocturnal sheen. I take a seat among bare heads and the hats, pinafores and smocks, panniers and baskets. We cross Gleisdreieck's iron web, and the abyss of the canal under Möckern Bridge, to Hallesches Tor.

For a while, I stand on the bridge, next to statues that attempt to allegorise commerce and agriculture. The true old Hallesches

Tor springs to mind, based on things I've read and etchings I've seen: the low city wall, more of a garden fence than a defence — it was less intended for protection than for the monitoring of foreigners and taxation, and making desertion difficult. The two pillars on either side of the gate were joined up above by an iron rod. Decorative stone vases. As long as it was light, the gates stood open. The customs collectors and dragoons guarding the gates sat playing cards until another herd of sheep came along. Then the collectors had their hands full with the slaughtering tax. Every herd that entered the city had to be counted. Both doors of the gates would be closed, with just a hatch open. And while man and beast pooled outside, just the bellwether would be let in. Then the others after him, one by one, across the extended foot of the counting customs collector. Looking out at the emptiness of the bridge and square, I imagine them amassing and rushing forward. But then, amid the wave of headscarves, caps, hemp baskets, and backpacks flowing from the elevated train, I see my friend, the young florist who I want to take along with me.

We cross the round plaza at Belle-Alliance-Platz[2] and head up Friedrichstraße to the entryway. The building is train-station-brown and boasts a municipal bear emblem over its keystone. In the courtyard passage's shop windows, a few bleached fake-flower arrangements are visible, the kind you see in French cemeteries. Inside the hall, my guide is greeted by half the world. A good woman from Zossen takes his basket for safekeeping, crouching behind her greens. Her neighbour says:

---

2   Now known as Mehringplatz.

'Two little girls were born near us in the night.' 'Fertile district you have there in Mariendorf,' says my companion. 'Well, now you've got to do your part too, Karl,' adds the woman from Zossen. A colleague carries out a sort of futures trading with Karl in passing and then asks him, 'Have any ciggies?' Karl gives him a cigarette. Those are rich people, the man gestures, all of Werder belongs to them and half of Treptow along with it. He hurries from booth to booth, selecting, negotiating, ordering, and taking orders. Tightly packed roses that arrived via airmail from Holland are stacked between creamy, chromatic piles of local autumn flowers. Negotiations are brisk, with a few wisecracks between the young men and old ladies for good measure.

The men also banter among themselves. They're quieter and more cautious with young women. But everyone here has that *ante meridiem* cheer. They're in good humour, despite all the ups and downs. Why, there was already frost last night. In Britz, all of the dahlias froze. The woman with the coffee pot and plum tart tells me about it as we take our breakfast standing up. Around here, you accept things with a grinning fatalism. I feel like a city gardener, as in the old days, when there were still many vegetable gardens and fields within the city walls. We walk a few steps over to the chrysanthemums in the potted-plant hall. This hall was added because the big one was already too full. But soon the whole complex won't be enough, and it will have to be relocated to the suburbs. An old cemetery gardener from Westend greets my companion. He looks disdainfully at the street vendors buying 'rubbish' — that is, B-grade goods — from the woman in the corner by the door. He's old-fashioned. The owner of a Tiergarten villa made a gift of the garden business to his father, who had worked for him as a gardener sixty years ago. We squeeze past arms laden with paper-packed potted violets and loosely bound chrysanthemums. The old cemetery gardener wants to bring the purchases to my companion's truck. He comes with us to a brandy bar across the street where we'll 'throw back' a few glasses. Outside, between the carts, wagons, and hulking nags, the street cleaners are already at work. We go back to the hall one more time to pick some things up. Everything is already being cleared away, while a few old ladies count money from their shrivelled purses, and boys from their pockets. Filth and waste doesn't lie around for long anywhere in Berlin. This city likes to clean up.

* * *

Now we've 'taken care of' vegetables and flowers. But we've still got meat to do. And so we're off to the Central Stockyard and Slaughterhouse in the east. The old livestock market, created in 1871, was located at Landsberger Tor.[3] Today a bit farther to the east, the gigantic complex has an area of nearly 120 acres with stalls, auction halls, slaughterhouses, and management buildings. It is bisected by Thaerstraße, traversed by service tracks, and bordered by ramps sloping up to the circle line. Its livestock train station includes fifteen kilometres of track and a large number of loading bays. But the first things I see are the people: clerks and veterinarians, cattle traders in long coats, agents, and

---

3   Now known as Platz der Vereinten Nationen.

industrial butchers in the exchange building. My guide tells me about the work of the commission, which determines the price, transport, medical examinations, and care of the animals, and often operates on a handshake basis. He shows me the halls corralled together one after the next: one for the cattle, another for sheep, and a gigantic hall for pigs, which accommodates fifteen thousand animals in its stalls. To the north, it reaches all the way to the railway ramp, where livestock arrives from the provinces. The narrow calf-hall stretches along that ramp. To the east are the stables, shipments of dung, areas for quarantined animals and the curing of hides, etc. On market days, the halls are opened, and cattle, calves, and sheep are driven over from the slaughterhouse and through the three gates.

The pigs meander along a dedicated route. We walk over to the slaughtering yard, then follow a herd of pigs trotting to a new slaughterhouse, an enormous red building. We see how, under the driver's rod, the brightly marked pink-grey backs and curly tails disappear into a hatchway. Now we're standing inside the broad hall. White steam rises from the scalding pots. The first little piggy wriggles out of the small wooden shed, walking toward its murderer quietly and trustingly. The butcher's a nice-looking boy in shirtsleeves. He strikes serenely with his axe, hitting the animal just behind its head. It lies down gently on its side. When another sympathetic-looking young man slits its throat, only its legs twitch. The next one is already waiting, and a third pushes in. I'm amazed that they don't squeal, neither before the shed nor under the axe. I keep looking at the face of the boy who dealt the blow. It's funny: the livestock trader from a moment ago, the agent, and the master butcher all looked more bloodthirsty than these youths, with their pale, delicate faces, who commit the murders … We enter the cattle slaughterhouse. There's a ritualistic corner there. The steer hangs head-down before the *shochet* who killed it. He has a pointy, protruding blackish-grey beard. In what painting have I seen that beard before? You must visit the sheep when they're being skinned. It's incredible how smoothly and cleanly it comes off. Once they're sliced open at a particular spot, a man who knows what he's doing can grip them gently under the fur and the coat glides off softly and without a trace. From beneath it emerges a creature of shining ivory. In general, things run very cleanly in this house of mass murder. Blood and horrors are quickly washed away; pluck, tripe, and 'odds and ends' are pushed aside. Soon, everything is clean and sparkling as a dance floor.

We wander from hall to hall, all the way to the entryway. The iron bars along the wall are part of an overhead crane; the hanging animals will be transported on its hooks. Another glimpse into the big yard of the meat market. Really I should've visited it in the early morning hours when it was seething with cars and people. The buildings of this peculiar settlement are of recent vintage and imposing stature. You can even visit the spacious refrigeration and freezing centre, with its galvanised sheet-iron cages of stored meat.

Should I forge on farther into the northeast today? There's a horse market in Weißensee. They sell saddle horses, along with old nags. And business is concluded with a handshake there too. Some other time.

The North

As much as I love our window displays in the west, with their ever-changing combinations, illuminations, and surprises, things get too extravagant for me in the week before Christmas. The masses of end-products in no sense justify their means; rather, they disgrace them. Gigantic 'feast baskets' brim with bottles of spirits, sausages, pineapples, and grapes bound up in shimmering ribbons on a bed of pine mulch. Beautiful presentations are offered for all price ranges, in order to spare the Berliners who 'never get around to anything' the trouble of assembling, bundling, and binding. The bookstores display their colourised rehashed fairytales for the darling little ones. Silver-sprayed pine branches lie between nickel and ironware, spruce needles peek out of shoes, tinsel snows down on undergarments. Things become more *Karneval*-esque where stalls are set up. You'll find inflatable squeaky rubber animals, and red-and-green plastic monkeys next to the Christmas-tree ornaments. A woman puts a small artificial bird on the sidewalk in front of her hut that makes a pecking motion while she says, 'The latest from the Leipzig Trade Fair.' When I stopped for a moment, her colleague said to me, 'Should we pack up one like that for you, Herr Boss?' This reverential salutation had strangely modern nuances. In earlier times, he would have said,

'*Herr Doktor*'. And in Munich, simply 'neighbour'.

I think that was at Leipziger Platz. The deeper into the city and the farther north I went, the more provincial and authentic the Christmas markets became. The items in the windows were no longer so dreadfully distinguished. In the area around Rosenthaler Tor, 'What we've got on offer' was to be read in bold font. And 'Discount when you buy three 25, 50, and 95'. And 'Goose breast the best holiday gift'. Little goose breasts were hanging in a row without any of the classic condiments. Carts lined up along the street were full of cheap, coarse gingerbread. Sometimes the warm wafting steam of a sausage stall interrupted the colourful bric-a-brac. I had been missing the touching microcosm of the Berlin Christmas market. But nowhere did I hear the children's cries of 'Ten-cent pocket calendars!' like in the old days. When we were children, they reminded our parents of orphans' cries from even earlier times: 'A wooden lamb for three pennies!' And where have the clowns gone with their string drums?

But even the modern era can't dispel the Christmas tree. Wherever the sidewalk opens onto a square, they're standing there for sale, handsome and poignantly scented. There are also tiny ones with three colourful candles. They say that nearby here yesterday a warehouse with a few hundred trees was plundered. Sentimental robbers! How do legal scholars interpret this type of theft? This heap of firewood with inestimable value. This unnecessary necessity. Even in the vilest taverns, haunted by evil plum-eyed witches, a little tree stands on the greasy tablecloth. And the Christ-child still competes with the radio.

Up Ackerstraße to Wedding. Even this sorry place has a touch of the Christmas forest and cheerful market, in the courtyard of the gigantic tenement building — in the first courtyard, since it has five or six, an entire city's worth of people are dwelling. All sorts of professions are represented, judging by the placards: Apostle Ministry, pumpernickel factory, ladies' and children's ready-to-wear clothing, metalworking, leather stamping, a bathing facility, clothing press, butcher ... and so on, and so many dressmakers, seamstresses, and coalmen living in the endless back and side buildings. A textbook example of the residential dungeon of yesteryear. In the first courtyard, three little boys walk through the rounded gateway. One of them holds a guitar, and the other two have candles that they blow out in the entryway. They go from courtyard to courtyard singing and playing Christmas songs, while holding the candles, which they have lit again.

At least the arched gateways give this urban squalor a face. Otherwise here in the north, just as in the proletarian parts of Schöneberg or Neukölln, it isn't evident from the outside just how much poverty they harbour within. The people don't wear colourful rags — which cloak the misery of the Mediterranean beggar in quiet consolation — but rather shabby middle-class *trachts* and scuffed soldier's coats from the infinite supplies of the war. The buildings' dilapidation is also somehow bourgeois. They stand in endless rows, window upon window, little balconies stuck on the front upon which potted plants eke out a paltry existence. To get a notion of the lives of the residents, you have to make your way into the courtyards: the sad first courtyard, and the sadder second. You must observe the sallow children loitering around, squatting on the steps of the back building's three, four, or more lightless entryways, stirring and grotesque creatures, as Heinrich Zille painted and drew them. Sometimes, they flock around a man with a barrel organ — who has better prospects of a handout here than in the more upper-class districts — or around Salvation Army singers with their red-ribboned hats and military-style coats, promising the poor of this world the riches of the hereafter. If you have the opportunity to climb the musty steps to the wretched kitchen / living room full of coal fumes, and to the bedrooms smelling sourly of infants, you'll 'learn' a thing or two.

This can all be seen in the faces of the men who emerge from the Wedding and Gesundbrunnen circle-line train stations in the evening and hurry home down the streets, or along the fences and construction sites, into desolation. But you have to gaze into them for a while. At first glance, these people betray very little. They seem just like anyone else, like those who have an easier, more direct path from emotion to expression. Perhaps these reserved people must gather all the more of their strength to struggle against the greatest enemy that humanity knows today.

Humboldthain: there are only a few older boys running around the playground. It's already too cold for the little ones who we saw here in the sandbox this summer. Even the infamous gambling bench normally occupied by unemployed men is empty today. In autumn, they played cards in the greenery with red and mottled handkerchiefs as a tablecloth, calling out numbers and rattling small change. The faces of the players were just as earnest and rapt above their collarless necks as those above the dress shirts in Monte Carlo.

Should I take the circle line to Landsberger Allee and then go to Friedrichshain to see the children at play? This time of year, you can see real winter sports in action there. They go sledding down the 'Kanonenberg' in the park, two or three to a toboggan.

Today, I'd rather head farther north into the great outdoors. From Badstraße, I can see a narrow stream between the houses. That's the good old Panke. Its course behind the tall tenement buildings on Karlstraße is even more secretive. Near its outlet into the Spree, there was once a well-appointed bathhouse, but now it's nothing more than a rather doleful trickle.

I see a tram that says: Pankow, Niederschönhausen. I jump aboard. Now I'm riding through this strange mixture of big city and garden town where you can find examples of everything imaginable, as well as the Schönhausen Palace park with its old oaks, and the Bürgerpark with its proud gated entryway. There are the usual suburban streets, and half-rural ones with dear, low-lying cottages built by those who moved out to the country nigh on one hundred years ago. In the shadows of genteel banking families' war-era villas, they built their shanties, brimming with children and poverty, and then their summerhouse colonies. Then we pass the little palace of Niederschönhausen in its park-enveloped solitude, completely abandoned and shuttered, the tall windows boarded up from within. Friedrich the Great lived there in the summertime with his spouse, poor Elisabeth Christine. Even if you could enter the palace, I suspect that you wouldn't find a trace of that poor forgotten soul.

The Northwest

Museums are to be found today on Invalidenstraße — one belonging to the Agricultural University, and a geological one for the natural sciences where you can marvel at the famous archaeopteryx and a range of his dinosaur friends, either as skeletons or replicas. They stand where Old Fritz established a mulberry plantation so that his invalids could cultivate silkworms. Just a little to the north, the Invalidenhaus stands today, which he erected 'laeso et invicto militi' — for the wounded yet unvanquished warriors. Back then, it stood in a desolate area that used to be called Sandscholle. The sand is said to have been heaped so high there against the city wall that you could ride over it and into the city. The entryway to the Invalidenhaus is beautiful, with an *oeil-de-boeuf* above a round-arched wooden door. There are cannon barrels lying in the courtyard, rusting relics from wars past. And many famous military men rest in peace in the cemetery next door. It's one of the old Berlin graveyards where you can still see a number of beautiful old tombstones. There are antique helmets on shields and modest stone vases on the tombstones of the highest-ranking commanders. You'll see Karl Friedrich Friesen's black cross, Gerhard von Scharnhorst's tall marble monument topped with a dying lion, the trophies over Hans Karl von Winterfeldt's grave, and the zinc plaque over the grave of Count Friedrich Tauentzien von Wittenberg. There's also a Prussian Neo-Gothic baldachin on one of the towers, which was created following Schinkel's design in the Royal Iron Foundry.

Wandering from stone to stone here is a pleasure; it's rare to find so many examples of the old Berlin cemetery monument cheek-by-jowl as they are here, monuments from the days of Schadow and Schinkel and the late Frederician period, which unified grace and severity in such a unique fashion. On Chausseestraße, at Prenzlauer Tor, and south of Hallesches Tor, as well as in a few other graveyards remaining in the old city, you can walk down similarly ivy-girded paths past the old art of the tombstone, the markers of both the famed and the forgotten. Unfortunately, you must often make your way past domes, baldachins, and vaulted halls whose 'tasteful' production in the 'best materials, at every price' developed into a booming business.

I found myself in this lovely little cemetery instead of going to the criminal court on the other end of Invalidenstraße to observe a court case for my personal enrichment. I did that once, many years ago. It was a blasphemy case in which the witnesses, judge, and accused all gave an excellent performance, and only the public prosecutor overacted dreadfully, employing an implausible comic-strip humour. I tried to convince myself I would make it to my destination today. The tram carried me past the former Hamburger Station, which looked so pleasantly useless (though there is a transportation museum inside). We passed Humboldtshafen, Lehrter Station, and the exhibition park. I caught a glimpse of the fortress-like prison complex with the gigantic tower, then I exited in front of the courthouse, where lions battle the snake of criminality. I crept along one side of the enormous pentagon as if sneaking out of school, and arrived at the welcoming grounds of the Kleiner Tiergarten. I watched the hustle and bustle at Bolle Dairy, where a herd of milk trucks — familiar to every Berlin child — drove up and parked, and boys and girls in blue aprons swung out from the back seats. If I'd really wanted to engage with local culture, I should have mingled with them, but instead I let myself be drawn northward through the grounds and into a street that intersects the long Turmstraße.

Then I walked into a very Berlin scene completely by accident. At the entrance to one of those restaurants named after a Hohenzollern that has Schultheiß or Patzenhofer on tap, some people were standing around. The clothing that peeked from under their coats hinted at the evening's festivities. Though I had been cowardly before the lion and the milkmaids, now I gathered my courage and walked into the anniversary party of a music club, which had organised an amateur performance. An operetta would be put on by some of the members. They sat at tables and were given coffee and cake. It was a Sunday afternoon. The performance began with a deep curtsey, a courtly curtsey from the old days such as you rarely see anymore. A lady took to the stage to recite the welcome speech. Then Herr Conductor-and-Composer turned to the 'highly esteemed public', alluding to the unavoidable limitations of 'dilettantes, who can only dedicate themselves to art in the leisure hours afforded by their professional activities'. The operetta was set in that special country of operettas somewhere between Vienna and the realm of the Turks, where so many countesses, *bon vivants*, gypsies, picturesque peasant-women, smugglers, and slick lieutenants make their home. The full-figured women of the chorus played the part both of country girls and elegant guests of a palace soiree. The main characters were heavily applauded after each solo and duet, and often had to repeat their performance; and not just the comic parts, but also the sentimental ones like 'Maiden, speak to me / Maiden, soon I must leave!' They'd earned it just as our most eminent opera singers do, those professionals who press their mistresses to their generous chests like a pair of bellows, while repeating how much they love them.

The director got his followers fired up to perform a Csárdás. It's a dance in which the performers alternately snap their fingers and plant their hands on their hips. But they also had a talent for sophisticated, waist-clasping slow dances, especially the waltz, which is the most beautiful of all dances, one of the songs informed us. And after the performance, the audience and artists alike danced in another room, where portraits of Wilhelm I and Friedrich III hung. But I didn't dare to horn in on this diversion.

On a curving path that snaked beneath railway viaducts and across bridges over the canal, I ended up at the point where Chausseestraße turns into Müllerstraße. I walked up that endless street for a while, which seemed both urban and suburban. Sidewalk salesmen were peddling a variety of goods on every corner and also in between. A young collarless fellow with long, deep lines in his sallow cheeks was hocking pamphlets with nude photos. He cried out: 'What is this? — Sexuality is what it is. And what is sexuality? Something entirely natural. What does a human being look like? Just like this, nothing else. We only feel embarrassed about it in front of others. If that weren't the case, anyone who isn't a moralist missionary would buy this ... And *you'd* better get out of here,' he paused to address a child. 'This isn't for you.'

A little farther, just past a bouquet of shirt cuffs and colourful children's pinwheels, a man set his walking stick and hat on the ground and stood contemplatively before them, which aroused the general curiosity. Then he pointed to his forehead, as if something had just occurred to him. A boy handed the stick to him. Then he screwed something into it, and hung up his hat, jacket, and coat on it. ''N armoire fer ten pennies,' he cried. Then he gave a speech to the crowd that had gathered around him. It was so lovely, I've tried to recall his verses:

> ''N armoire fer ten pennies!'
> I c'n sense yer silent question:
> What'll I do with all my baggage?
> You too c'n lay up yer posessions
> in the same way that I've managed.
> In the woods they ain't any benches;
> the grass'll stain yer breeches green,
> an' there's no closets at the beaches —
> how'll ye keep your clothes all clean?

After that, I saw a man dressed in a white coat like in a clinic. Was he selling the real glass diamonds, or the universal stain remover, or the Continental glue? He had a microphone and amplifier next to him, because he apparently felt that his own voice was not enough. It droned from his table like a rampaging ventriloquist. I even saw the old Fabric Shield here again, whose sales spiel Hans Ostwald[1] recorded so wonderfully:

> We've tested every possible use of this Fabric Shield and commissioned reports on it … Take the flexible turn-down collar, open it, insert the stiff Fabric Shield, then fold it shut. So … how does it fit? Firm and elegant. And if your collar is normally rumpled within a few hours, now you can wear it for eight days. Anyone wearing this Fabric Shield will constantly outdo the competition.

The newest tie clip also makes an appearance. 'Just one motion — neither pre-sewn ties nor typical neckties will shift in your collar. The tie clip, perfected. We take good care of our ties!' Over there is the book cart. It has fewer customers here than in higher-class areas, though it still gets a decent reception. Some people read the page-turners and magazines while standing. The friendly custodian of the cart lets them do as they like. Some of them come by every day to read a little bit more. A lending library on wheels!

Over there where the cobblestones are torn up, children have built mountains in the sand with tunnels through them. Their

---

1   Hans Ostwald (1873–1940) was a journalist who wrote about outsiders and the lowest classes of Berlin society in the first half of the 20th century.

mothers watch over them from the neighbouring buildings, leaning on their window cushions.

Beautiful wooded paths and waterways lead through here on their way from Spandau to Tegel. But to really understand the strange limbo that is the outskirts, the city limits, the land that's 'just waiting', I'd suggest taking the route covered by the tram, and its environs. In this problematic zone, the transition between city and countryside is rarely as gradual as in a village or small town. In general, the rows of houses just end with a windowless wall. And whatever is in the fields, whether tiny or towering, only makes the emptiness emptier: sheds, barbed-wire fences, stacked clay pipes, the chimney stacks of a single factory with a warehouse and a set of tracks for transporting goods. But the populace of Berlin instinctively fears and resists anything chaotic or indefinite. It works eagerly to fill all empty spaces. Where plots of land stood open for a time, it placed its summerhouse colonies, quaintly manicured sites with a speck of house and yard. There is one vegetable bed and flowerbed for each family, which become a blossoming whole, one giant bed, a garden of a thousand blooms. Although — or perhaps because — this world's existence is only fleeting (constantly under threat from the city's expansion, and developers' desire to build), these summer cottages and gardens don't seem provisory or nomadic at all. They look like a lasting paradise, a blessed realm of the proletariat and petit bourgeoisie. The menfolk sowing in their shirtsleeves, the mothers watering flowers, and the daughters shelling peas all seem as if they've never done anything else their entire lives. Gardening here doesn't seem like leisure time for people who pedal sewing machines, pull wires, hammer poles, operate cranes and turbines, pack light goods, and load heavy freight during the day. They seem to have lived all their lives under a canopy of climbing roses and sunflowers, dealing exclusively in parsley, carrots, and beans. One imagines that their idyllic work only comes to an end when interrupted by celebrations with their neighbours.

Notices posted by the Recreation Gardening Club invite us to an Italian evening. The children are promised 'Uncle Pelle at your service',[2] and the Waldesgrüne Colony will offer musical entertainment for the evening. We're south of Müllerstraße now, but in Berlin there are countless such garden plots that, taken together, form a green strip always trying to clasp itself like a belt around the city, but which is displaced and punctured here and there. And a few branches still grow within the city — sometimes parts of this 'green belt' remain for a while among the sea of houses, and, together with the public parks and manicured squares, they are the city's green delight. There are a few parks here in the northwest, as in the north and the south, that soften the city limits and ease the horrors of life there. Where the bleak Rehberge once stood, a sandy desert interrupted only by rifle ranges and heaps of debris, there are now broad lawns that stretch to the edge of a pine forest, slopes dotted with poppies and wild rose scrub, and snowy fields of daisies. Children in bathing suits run across brown sand. The bigger ones tumble on the athletic fields, and the very little ones

---

2 Adolf Rautmann (1863–1937), known as 'Onkel Pelle', was a circus performer and beloved Berlin children's entertainer.

are pushed by their mothers across the smooth gravel. Old men hunched over their canes sit on the high benches, where they can see far over the graveyard and the water, all the way to the bricks of Siemensstadt and beyond Plötzensee.

There's also a lovely garden realm north of Müllerstraße, known as Schiller Park. Instead of sticking to the tram route here, if I were to press deeper south past the Spandau Ship Canal into Jungfernheide, near Westend I would come across a big public park. But now I'm taking the tram through the village of Wittenau, where small-town streets recede before factories and barns, and life is once again 'strictly business'. When you approach it from this side, Tegel also starts out looking downright urban. There's the prison, gas works, and the big Borsig-machine factory and iron foundry. The gateway and the parts of the complex that we drive by already look a bit old-fashioned. But behind them, the new twelve-storey tower soars, a spotlessly proud, angular steeple of labour. Finally, we enter the realm of bushes and gardens. I exit the tram and walk into the park named after the Humboldts. Schinkel made the palace for them out of a hunting lodge that once belonged to the Great Elector. Its rows of windows are dreamy and distinguished — statues of gods in the niches, Greek inscriptions up above. There's a light in one of the windows. Now one of the windows in the big hall lights up. So it's not merely a lost piece of the past, this elegant building. People live there, for whom the statues and paintings, and maybe even the furnishings of the palace, are family possessions, their 'heritage and grace'. I walk down a park path bathed in warm light, up to the burial plots of the Humboldts and their descendants. A tall column rises above the ivory-clad headstones with a marble statue of Hope.

After that, I didn't want to go straight back into the city, so I walked for a long time along well-trodden sandy paths between gaunt spruce and Scots pines near the Saatwinkel recreation area. A typical Brandenburg mixture of sand flats and dense, stunted forest. Finally, a fence appeared, and behind it an empty restaurant with a garden. A faded notice on the brick wall: 'Welcome to the woodland palace.'[3] And more legibly on the timber sign: 'Continental Construction A.G.' The street leads across the Spandau Canal, and finally to buildings and tram tracks.

I rode home through Siemensstadt, past the tower buildings: the Blockwerk, Schaltwerkhochhaus, and Wernerwerk, the last with its clock tower whose face beams the hour across a great distance.

---

3   Hessel is referring to the extremely popular restaurant Blumeshof, which was once the hunting estate of Friedrich Wilhelm IV.

Friedrichstadt

A November afternoon. Silvery-grey light over Schiffbauerdamm. Across the Spree on Reichstagufer, I see a row of
houses capped by the Friedrichstraße station, behind which the
smoke-thin contours of both nearer and more distant domes
dissolve in the air. In Felix Eberty's *Memories of an Old Berliner*, I
read about how this area looked hundreds of years ago when he
walked here as a boy with his private tutor and looked across to
the other shore, which was completely lined with gardens back
then. There were leafy walkways and gazebos, some Chinese,
some Greek in style. They shimmered through the gaps in the
greenery, and little Eberty thought they were the quintessence
of everything wonderful. He asked who lived in these darling
little palaces, and the tutor answered, earnestly: *over there is
heaven, where good children go if they're extremely polite and pleasing
to their parents on earth. Exquisite angels with golden wings wait for
them there, ready to play the loveliest of games.*

Yes, back then it must have been beautiful on the other side.
Those were the days when the lower end of Dorotheenstraße
was still called Letzte Straße, where Rahel Varnhagen loved to
go walking. Only the palace and the Monbijou garden remain
from that time, along with a few houses in the neighbourhood,
and a few things here and there near Hackescher Markt.

Otherwise, the area is anything but a fairytale. However, there is a real fairytale palace, built on a swampy low spot. It's called Großes Schauspielhaus,[1] and it used to be a circus, and before that a market hall. Its interior was once home to rash trick riders and teetering clowns, and then to Max Reinhardt's Theban choir, which stormed the steps of King Oedipus's palace. It now hosts the *Thousand and One Nights*, as well as the thousand and one legs of the great revue shows. It is a wonderful children's theatre for adults, and that is the highest praise I know to give, for these creations satisfy our more mature desires, as well as our childlike desire for a fairytale world on a dream stage. Its masters have created a new genre between revue and operetta: a dancing image that is danced to pieces, dancing music danced to bits, either in the enormous auditorium here or on the smaller adjoining stages.

The best of our performing artists have taken part. I don't mean the celebrated opera singers who infuse the cheerful dancing and decor with their vocals, I mean Max Pallenberg and Fritzi Massary. We saw the arching girders and tapering columns of Titipu, the fairytale city of *The Mikado*. There were undulating paper lanterns, porcelain trees, and — between the dragon and colourful garden, between peacocks and dwarves — a dancing chorus in oilcloth and silk. And Pallenberg as Ko-Ko was wickedly innocent, roguishly scuttling down the stairs, squatting like a porcelain figure before the porcelain

---

1   Großes Schauspielhaus has been known as Friedrichstadtpalast since 1949. Today, its performances are of a genre more popular and less culturally significant than the influential Reinhardt and Erik Charell pieces Hessel describes (which themselves were rather popular).

trees, grinding rhyme tween his teeth and spitting them out. And Massary, that w~~een his teeth and spitting them~~ among the dress trains, cor~~s~~erful woman, sang her chanson the velvet draperies and verdant p~~ts~~ waists, and gigantic hats, and maxixers. She sang with searing s~~ty~~ the swaying waltzers exuberance, with Spartan artifice and qu~~ering~~ fervour, retained and released with every gesture.

A few streets down from Großes Schauspielhaus we saw *The Threepenny Opera*, that old comedy of defiant squalor, that ballad of rags, whistled and sung with entirely new rhymes.

Over there past the Weidendammer Bridge, they're rehearsing for the evening's music and dancing at the Komische Oper and in Admiralspalast. Eberty's enchanting gardens are only to be found in the stage sets; during the day, it's not very cheerful around here. Beyond the Schiffbauerdamm, the medical district begins, with larger and smaller clinics, specialist bookstores, and surgical and orthopaedic window displays. But right in the middle of this sheltered hinterland, you'll find our Deutsches Theater and the *Kammerspiele*. I was recently there, in an exquisite orchestra seat from which I could see the makeup on the actors' faces. I enjoyed brilliant performances in an American drama about artists. During the intermission, and even during the play, now and again I had to steal a glance up at the centre seats of the second mezzanine. My peers, do you still remember? It was in seats 19 to 26. You would go to the ticket office a few days before the longed-for production to get the best seats. You got to sit right under Devrient and Döring's medallions on the ceiling. You go ... ...e Josef Kainz![2]

The theatre was immense ... ...portant and central to our lives back then. Why isn't i... ...t way anymore? Is it a question of our age, or did somethi... ...hange with the times? Berliners used to be great theatre ...nusiasts. How they raved over Henriette Sontag and S...meling! His marble bust stood on the king's desk and hung as a cheap lithograph print in the rooms of day labourers. Now, the theatre still plays a large role in the life of our city. In the tram as well as in private company, a great deal is said about the stage. But for all of their engagement with the problems of stage direction, with the theatre's renewal of the old, and its revolutionary tendencies, Berliners have nonetheless never become a true people of the theatre, as have the Viennese, for example. And that isn't only owing to the current state of the dramatic arts; it's also due to our local Berlin character.

The Berliners, especially the better ones, which I don't designate by level of education but rather by degree of authenticity, are somewhat wary of anything that they immediately like. And so, as an audience they lack the naiveté of the pure pleasure-seekers. Moreover, unlike the Parisians, who arrive at the theatre after dinner satisfied, and with the prospect of a pleasant continuation of the conversation at the table, the Berliners come hungry and critical. Then they are offered more or less the best of direction and stage performance in existence today. There are so many names, I haven't any desire to list them. But look at the audience! Their faces are

---

2   Ludwig Devrient, Theodor Döring, and Josef Kainz were renowned 19th-century German actors.

both sullen and politely devout. When they dislike something, they're filled with indignation; they don't laugh at the shortfall, but rather become angry that they were forced to sit through it. And when they are filled with enthusiasm about something, it produces another sort of indignation against an imaginary opponent who is not enthusiastic enough. Are they ever happy from the bottom of their hearts in the big theatre? As happy as the audiences watching the suburban stages? Are they ever at home in their leisure?

Dorotheenstraße. By a stroke of luck, the Dorotheenstadt Church is open. Finally, I can see the tomb of the king's son, Count von der Mark, who died at just nine years of age. It's Johann Gottfried Schadow's most famous early work, the sleeping boy with sword and garlands. The heathen Fates are above him in a semicircle; death has opened the doors to the Christian church for them. Across from the church, Schlüter's last creation, Villa Kamecke, stands amid its taller urban neighbours. It first served as a minister of state's personal Buen Retiro, but strangely, for the past hundred and fifty years it has belonged to a Freemason lodge, the Royal York. The projecting centre portion seems to be in gentle motion, which is continued more emphatically in the gesturing figures on the roof — two of these statues frolic like dancers. And a wonderful mischief plays out in some of the side windows: carved stone curtains. Contemporaries thought that it was 'a thoroughly delightful retreat, completed in accordance with the newest construction techniques'. An art historian writing in the 1870s was of the opinion that the whimsy and caprices that had made the building seem picturesque when it was located in a half-rural setting now gave it an outlandish air on this urban street. But an art arbiter of *our* day, Max Deri, said that it was the only 'truly "European" historical building' that Berlin has. It's very tempting to step into this enchanted pavilion, but it's only open to members of the lodge. As far as the interior atrium goes, I'll have to be satisfied with Friedrich Nicolai's description: 'Schlüter has depicted the four continents in plaster over the four doors. On the wall are four small bas-reliefs representing the four main virtues of a minister: Vigilance, Wisdom, Caution, and Discretion.' In Nicolai's day, the garden reached all the way to the Spree, and he records that 'a great parlour made up of tall chestnut and elm trees is noteworthy, as is a pleasingly situated scrub-covered hill, and the view of the fields dotted with trees on the opposite side has a rustic charm'.

On the other end of Dorotheenstraße, behind the library and the university, I know of a square with a few old buildings and a colossal bust of Hegel — his gently menacing face steadfastly claims that the real is rational. Particularly familiar to me from my student days is the seminar building, whose age-tinted walls were ornamented with delicate friezes and reliefs. But I don't want to go that far today, so I'll have to miss out on the Maritime Museum, as well as the two gentlemen's busts in the wall. Instead, I'm going to conduct an investigation into the nature and manufacture of beet sugar. I turn onto Friedrichstraße in front of the Wintergarten theatre. I glance into the cafe of the central hotel, where truly notable people often sit at this hour of the afternoon: foreign businessmen, ladies travelling alone, family groups from the Levant, artists, dubious *bon vivants*; a perplexing *post meridiem* gathering. Since Wintergarten, Berlin's hallowed variety theatre, was recently renovated and reopened to much celebration, it is befitting to contemplate its history. As the name suggests, it was first simply intended to be a place of peace and relaxation for the hotel guests. The boxes were so configured that they could be conveniently reached from the hotel rooms. Sitting in them, the guests looked down into the lush creeping plants, laurel trees, and palms, into dripstone caves and aquariums, and in the middle of it all, under the gas light of the 'sun burner' and candelabras, was a small stage where a bit of musical comedy occasionally took place. But then came the era of those two directors whose names represent an established company moniker: Dorn & Baron. The days of Loie Fuller, the Barrisons, Otero, Cléo de Mérode, and all of the European stars of the trapeze and high wire. A foreign cosmos close at hand, the starry sky on the blue ceiling bathed the Berliners in the sensational. What was on offer here was 'colossal'. And today, to employ the current superlative, it's 'enchanting'.

★ ★ ★

Friedrichstraße. It was once the centre of Berlin's sinfulness. The narrow sidewalk was carpeted in light, and the dangerous girls strutted there as if on silk. As was the style of the time, they had an upright, prancing gait, which became an atrocious mockery of itself as soon as they opened their mouths and spoke in the vernacular of the city. Their caste-type separation from society, the sinful lustre of their fake jewels and real squalor, all of the contradictions so close together sent my young imagination to work at the sight of these wicked fairies. They wore feathered hats like the princess who had exiled them from their secret places and onto the street, on the high-minded advice of her small-minded ministers. The image and embodiment of all of this is now history, little of which haunts Friedrichstraße today. Its nightlife has long since been overshadowed by the boulevard to the west. What remains of it is of greater interest to our country cousins than to Berlin's decadent set. There are a few bars where the youth can still ironically study how earlier generations had their fun. But now in the afternoon, when just a few of the clubs are illuminated, some of their entryways and windows are as intriguing as theatre backdrops. A particular sort of advertising blooms here. Doormen and guards pin up notices touting interesting bars, hubs of nightlife, sophisticated but discreet international dance performances, even nude sculptures with Pilsator on tap in the original Kunstlerkeller.

Recently one of these locales held informative lectures by 'sexual ethicists' who argued against the latest educational pamphlets and sought to justify various erotic endeavours and possibilities, to claim 'new soil' for our browbeaten and repressed instincts. But that's not until nighttime. Meanwhile, we could see the big five-o'clock program, 'the eight capers of famed comedian Sascha So-and-so'. But it's better to go into one of the small confectioner's cafes, where those who will later enjoy the nightlife sit sleepily in the afternoon, circulating opinions among themselves about the state of business and life in general. You could learn a lot about the world and about

Berlin there. The teatime dances in Friedrichstadt are also at their most educational at the hour before things really get started. Then, in the twilight next to the instruments still in their cases, the ballerina nibbles her snack while chatting to the cloakroom woman or the bartender. Valiant researchers that we are, we really should enter certain bars on the side street before noon, when the grottoes are being cleared out! 'Weißes Meer' gleams on the aproned belly of a fat doorman with a chef's hat on his head. He welcomes guests into a well-known bar where wheat beer is on tap. These days, that's a specialty. In earlier days, wheat beer with or without syrup (raspberry juice) tamed Berlin's thirst.

In the quieter streets of the older part of the city, you can still find a few of the true old wheat-beer taverns. There, you sit at plain wooden tables in front of broad goblets under portraits of the old Kaiser and the crown prince of yesteryear, and of Bismarck, Roon, and Moltke. But here in Friedrichstadt, these barrooms and cellars were crowded out half a century ago by the beer palaces and cathedrals, which are now coming into a historical venerability of their very own. Laforgue describes them as new tourist attractions. The towers and spires of these *curiosités architecturales* stand out to him, and he speaks of an ordinance enacted by a magistrate, which had to prevent them from towering even higher; otherwise, in the end, Berlin's beer towers may have grown to Babylonian proportions. He delights in the al fresco paintings outside and in. 'The style of these establishments,' he writes, 'is what you would call German Renaissance. They have wood panelling on the ceiling and walls, and the posts are also painted, and shelves run all the way around the room where all kinds of vessels for the containment of beer are lined up, made of porcelain, stoneware, metal, and glass from every era.'

For how long this colossal version of Nuremberg will hold its own against the ever-changing illuminated advertisements that smooth and efface Berlin's facades, I don't know. In any case, it's already historical, as is its contemporary, the Kaisergalerie, modelled on the Parisian arcades. I am unable to enter that building without experiencing the chill of decay and the nightmare anxiety of not being able to find a way out.

I've hardly passed the shoe shiner and newspaper stand at the archway when a mild bewilderment ensues. One window promises me daily dancing and a certain Meyer who knows how to start the fire, but where is the entrance? Next to the ladies' hairdresser is another display: postage stamps and the strangely named utensils of the collector: stamp hinges with guaranteed acid-free gum, and celluloid perforation gauges. 'Look out! Woollen jackets!' the writing on a nearby glass display case bellows at me, but the associated business is located somewhere else entirely. I spin around, nearly bumping into a mutoscope[3] in the process, in front of which a poor lonely schoolboy, folder under his arm, stands pitifully engrossed in 'Scene in the Bedroom'.

So many display windows all around me, and so few people. The renaissance that is embodied in these high brown arches

---

3   A mutoscope was a coin-operated motion picture device that showed a series of image frames to a single viewer.

is ever more out-dated; the panes of the gallery are clouded with the dust of days that can no longer be wiped away. The displays are more or less the same as twenty years ago. Trinkets, souvenirs, pearls, handbags, thermometers, rubber goods, postage stamps, rubber stamps. The only new addition is the Telefunken radio shop with its persuasive sign: 'A touch of the hand — and Europe plays for you'. At the optician's, you can study the entire manufacturing progression of a pair of glasses, from caterpillar to butterfly, so to speak, on an instructive sheet. 'The Development of the Human Being' peeks out from the Anatomical Museum, but I'm too appalled by it. I linger in front of 'Mignon, delight of all the world'; a pocket lantern in whose light a young couple's happiness is revealed; Knipp-Knapp cufflinks, which are undoubtedly the best; Diana air rifles, which certainly are a credit to the goddess of the hunt. I recoil from the grinning skulls that are the grim liquor glasses in an ivory dinner service. The clownish jockey's face on a handmade wooden nutcracker rests above a 'musical' toilet-paper holder. Milk bottles await the members of the 'Association of Former Nurslings', but filled with liquor! And if they're smokers, they'll find their 'healthful pipe stems' in puzzling proximity to the rubber dolls, which sit enthroned next to hygienic underpants labelled 'Discreet and convenient use'. I want to stand a while by the comforting yellow-amber pipe stems from the 'first and oldest amber store in Germany', but the anatomical beauty from the museum keeps on squinting over at me. Beneath her naked flesh, her skeleton is visible like a corset. Her painted organs, heart, liver, and lungs swim in the emptiness that surrounds her

... I turn from her to the white-frocked doctor who is bending over the abdominal cavity of an anaesthetised blonde. I flee before I have to learn about reconstructing the nose using skin from the arm. I'd rather stand before the book-and-stationery shop that has pamphlets about sensuality and the soul and a woman's rights in love, about parlour magicians and masters of card games — a shop full of things that will win the admiration of any company you find yourself in.

The gallery turns a broad corner, and chairs, tables, and potted palms appear belonging to a restaurant that describes itself as strictly kosher. The portrait-painter's studio, on the contrary, seems to be strictly *treif*. Beyond the carpeted entryway, you can see the artist himself, bearded, painting the president of the Reich. Hindenburg sits in his parlour, a dog lying at his feet, and between him and the painter is a painting in which he's depicted once again, only this time without the dog; and all of this is also only a painting — it's confusing. As are the enlarged photographs all around. You see, here you can have any photo made into a painting. No time-consuming portrait posing. Many testimonials by prominent figures. In a printed letter, the painter addresses us passers-by and explains that, unlike modern portrait painters, who have caused such a confusion of taste in Friedrichstadt, he has taken Goethe's notion that 'nature and art are but one at heart' as his precept. A young girl and a matron from the provinces pause in front of his many beauties with dog and sunroom, his decorated chests and dignified beards. So as not to interrupt their admiration, I turn my attention to a competing shop a few windows down, with 'original paintings by an academically trained artist at prices not to be matched'. The eye meanders from original autumn and spring scenes to the walls of Rothenburg to the famed blind man in the field, and a popular escaped female slave. But I was being watched during my observation. 'You can have that straightaway by us,' said a voice next to me, and I looked into the face of a little old man with a sparse beard. He winked at the next window down, where partially clothed girls with exposed stockings and camisole straps busied themselves in original etchings. To augment my knowledge, I should have allowed myself to become involved in a conversation with him. But it's too appalling here under the flashing artificial lights and slinking shadows. I let him creep instead over to a group of dubious lads in sweet little ties, for whom he demonstrates tricks with a pocket mirror.

The entire centre of the Galerie is empty. I hurry to the exit, sensing the ghostly crowds of days gone by, whose lecherous gazes cling to the glass jewels, undergarments, photos, and advertisements of earlier bazaars. I exhale in front of the windows of the big travel agency at the exit: the street, freedom, the present!

Dönhoffplatz[1]

I stood at the feet of the gigantic stone women who watch over the entrance to the Tietz department store on Leipziger Straße. In one hand, I held my loot: Gustav Langenscheidt's 1878 *A Natural History of the Berliner*. Like the resident of a small village sauntering down the quietest street of his hometown, I leafed through the pages of this enlightening book right in the middle of cosmopolitan traffic, frequently jostled, and immediately came upon a magnificent quotation. I read it on the mirror-smooth asphalt, under incandescent light, in 'Silhouette of Berlin, 1788':

> So broad and fine as the streets may be at first glance, at times the pedestrian is bewildered as to how he should guard himself against swiftly moving carriages, against muck and gutters. The walkway intended for pedestrians should, as in any other civil society, run along the buildings, but that's been rendered nearly impossible by their access drives. At each moment, the pedestrian is hindered and forced to cross the gutters onto the causeway. Nowhere is this incommodiousness more visible than on Leipziger Straße, one of the most beautiful in all Berlin.

---

1   Dönhoffplatz is now known as Marion-Gräfin-Dönhoff-Platz.

Presumably, it is Alte Leipziger Straße, next to Hausvogteiplatz near Raules Hof, that is intended here, but I want to enjoy the text in light of my current position on the new Leipziger Straße.

Moreover, there are tall stone stairs in front of the buildings. In inclement weather, it is inordinately muddy in the middle of the causeway, and there are countless holes in the cobblestone paving itself, due in part to the sandy soil, in part to the negligence of the pavers and their overseers. Because the unduly large stones lie amid a great quantity of small and angular pebbles, there is the ever-present danger of catching one's toe and falling to the ground. It is true that, as one might expect, gutters have been laid on either side of the causeway, and yet in a manner that they form a new and dangerous sort of drawbridge. Some of these deep gutters lie directly before the entrances to the buildings, and are overlaid with boards. Thus, should one attempt to walk along the buildings in the evening, every ten to fifteen paces one stumbles over a drive or stairs which, additionally heightening the peril, are surrounded by a little runnel. Should you stride heartily across the boards covering this gutter, before you know it you will at once have tumbled, three, even four feet deep into the gutter; but should you walk in the middle of the causeway, at the hasty approach of one or even several carriages, you won't know where to turn, for along the gutters there lie high and muddied piles of rubbish. To jump over them is dangerous, for they are steeply sloping and deep; and yet one must venture a resolution at random, or be run over by a carriage. Native Berliners are accustomed to these inconveniences, they also know the byways better than the foreigner, who would never, in any case, anticipate such a drawbridge. Road construction of this sort has something misanthropic about it, because the only people who seem to have been given any consideration at all are the rich ones who travel in coaches. Which is to say nothing of the nocturnal lighting, which up to this point has been heartily drab, although plenty of lanterns are burning. These are fashioned and positioned in such a manner that they only spread a sort of luminous shadow, which does no good at all.

I enjoy it heartily to imagine this critical observer of our fair city hopping querulously from stone to stone, casting disapproving glances sideways at the natives skilfully navigating the byways … We can read what the lighting was like in the 1820s in Eberty. Back then, 'at great intervals, the occasional oil lamp swung from the middle of an iron chain strung across the street. In the wind they made a melancholy creaking, and spread such meagre light that most people went out at night with a lantern in their hand, or had them carried for them … Men in clothing befouled with grease cleaned the lamps …' As for the paving of the 1840s, old Ludwig Pietsch recalls that often, in order to move about at all, one was very dependent on what was then the only means of public transportation: 'the second-class carriage, whose time-honoured form remains unchanged to this day'. The elder among us can still remember the last representatives of this species of vehicle, with their red and yellow wheels and warped bodies, the coachman's bristly beard and his blue ulster coat.

To my right, the broad Dönhoffplatz is packed with trams, cars, and groups of people, and since I've lapsed into olden times, I imagine it as it was when it was still a square in front of the old Leipzig Gate, and later an exercise and parade grounds for the regiment commanded by General Dönhoff. Where today the beautiful colonnades by Carl von Gontard close off the square toward Spittelmarkt, there used to be a moat traversed by the Spital Bridge. Friedrich the Great had it built, and cleared away the many shacks and scrub that had been a sanctuary for outlaws. He also had many grand buildings built around Dönhoffplatz. Of these, the palace of Chancellor von Hardenberg remained standing until the turn of the century. It later became the Prussian House of Representatives, and in 1904, it was cleared away to make room for a modern commercial building. Only his monument reminds us of the chancellor's era — on the southern side of the square, it turns its back to the stone sculpture of Baron von Hardenberg as if to an enemy, and von Hardenberg stares sullenly at the trams on Leipziger Straße. Dönhoffplatz was also once a fairground packed full of booths. And before the stone monument was erected, an obelisk towered in the centre as a mile marker on the path to Potsdam. There was a big pool and fountain in front of it with a lion that spouted water, which the Berliners called the 'Water Cat'. They would say:

When the wild cat
On our Dönhoffplatz
Begins to spout,
You know in Berlin
Soon spring will be about.

Street urchins played around the Water Cat and its pool, and maidservants sat with little children on its steps and on the rim of the pool, knitting and chattering, as you can see in all of the old illustrations.

But enough about the old days. I walk across the roadway and arrive at the entrance to the theatre where I want to check what's on today. The Stettin Singers![2] Once again, something time-honoured. But since it still exists, I go inside.

The flowers on the wall in the stairway — when could they have been painted? There's something about them you could describe as muffled art-nouveau. The tall red posts that support the auditorium and the fading splendour of its ceiling suggest this building has a heyday that lies even further in the past. From the shape of the lamps and candelabras, it can be deduced that it must have been in the days of gaslight. Yes, back then this was the variety theatre par excellence, and even members of the highest court society came here.

A big glass cabinet near the bar displays relics of another past. Inside are wax figurines of the Singers' comic mascots — the tall gaunt man and the short fat one, both in colourful uniform and guardsmen's pants, with tall shakos on their heads. From the days of these singers until the present, a hallowed custom has been preserved: the performers here are exclusively male. Even in the last play, the female roles — from the wife of the district court justice to the servant girl — were acted by men, just as in old Greek and old English theatre.

---

2   Hessel is at the Reichshallentheater. The Stettin Singers performed there regularly for half a century.

This place is also important for the late flowering of the German male vocal ensemble. The quartet of esteemed gentlemen in tailcoats were the foundations of the very concept, and their humorous couplets and genre skits are merely an intermezzo. They can also be cheerful, by the way, these esteemed gentlemen. Only the prudent man at the Bechstein piano can keep a straight face at their assortment of surprises. But the audience becomes very pious — these family men and women, and all of our Ernas and Almas who sing such lovely melodies to themselves in the courtyards while washing up — when the four of them raise their voices a cappella, singing about love that lives only in the heart and that's still as night and deep as the sea, or at least should be. The singers stand motionless, their music books at their chests. Only their heads turn a little to one another at times, when the tenor is reading the cue from the eyes and lips of the bass, or the bass from the baritone.

After such purely musical pleasures, one also wants a feast for the eyes. The *Dream Pictures* take care of that 'by popular demand'. Those are folk songs brought to life, sung and depicted before a framed and exceedingly mountainous backdrop. Cloud-like gauze conceals and then reveals all manner of old German landscapes and situations. In them, a costumed man sings 'In einem kühlen Grunde' and 'Im Wald und auf der Heide', sometimes alone, sometimes echoed by a companion. From verse to verse, and sometimes even from one line to the next, the pictures change: if the beloved's hat must fly from his head at the bridge before the gate, before you know it, the corresponding storm and darkened landscape have risen up. And if now we see a potbellied silk-cloaked scholar, then in the next verse he'll be the travelling companion of a grass-green huntsman or a little grandmother in her wintry cottage. That's not a flour-dusted baker's assistant, but rather a grey-clad young man hastily making off with a fustian bundle under his arm. But in the next picture, after the vineyard and the sounds of the forest, our emotions are aroused by a gigantic lyre wreathed in undulating flames, above which a message descends: 'God save the German song!'

And as we're clapping, the performers suddenly grab trombones and trumpets and play us an exit march!

The Newspaper District

Farther south in Friedrichstadt there are a few imposing buildings, old fortresses of the intellect, renovated and expanded, inviting with their wide windows, threatening with their stone balustrades. Enticing yet defensive; beautiful, dangerous buildings. They belong to legendary kings and royal families, known as Ullstein, Mosse, and Scherl.[1] When our last little revolution broke out, like the other kings, the newspaper kings were also driven from their castles. In the palace courtyards, pots of pork and beans boiled over campfires, shots were fired from the rooftops, and spiked soldiers' boots clattered across the floors of the editorial rooms. But the newspaper kings returned much more quickly than the other monarchs. Once again their chariots stand in their courtyards, full of paper ammunition, and their ladies-in-waiting tiptoe through the editorial rooms, fleet-footed secretaries and typewriter girls.

The castle gates are open in welcome. The doormen convivially admit us with our queries and manuscripts. An elevator whisks us to the upper stories. Many young boys man the reception. They know some of us already, though we're not really employed by the house. Oh, we don't want access to

---

1 Three prominent German media companies.

the serious departments responsible for politics, business, and local concerns. Ultimately, our place is in the entertainment supplements. We jot down the names of the All Powerful whom we desire to see. An ephebe drifts off with the note, and we sit at the long table or on the bench along the wall. We see familiar faces, without really knowing the people to whom they belong. This includes many women, some of them rather shy and anxious. Those are the ones who write the saucy, cosmopolitan gossip pieces. We watch the net next to the door, which catches the capsules that fall from the tube. This is what I imagine papal bulls look like. They must be important telegrams or other secrets more important than our 'delightful little tidbits'.

Once we've sat patiently for a while, a lad comes along with the message: the potentate is not on the premises, or is in a meeting. But do try calling tomorrow morning. ('And call upon me in the day of trouble.') A friendly woman drifts over to those who wait so desperately. She raises our hopes but does not give in to our desires. She often takes the manuscript from an author's trembling hands, though one would have *so* liked to tell the sovereign about it directly: more of the same could be produced, if it's the right thing; or perhaps something would have to be different about it. One would like to talk to him, should he have a few moments' time, about a series ... Oh, but really you're just glad that this angel is taking the papers and promising to lay them at his hand. Sometimes you actually *are* led into the sovereign's chambers. You walk long halls, trailing behind the surefooted boy, who exchanges news and quips with you on the way, glancing back from time to time to see if you're still back there. Safely arrived, you generally find the Desired One surrounded by other giants of the realm. They speak with each other in a light and confident tone. You sit there, hardly capable of gathering your courage to bring up the little thing in the presence of these disseminators of intellect. They're friendly with you. They'll look over what you've written without delay. But they won't be able to find a slot for it so quickly. There's already so much in the queue. The time-sensitive things must go first of course. The fact that they aren't time-sensitive at all, why that's the very appeal of your little creations, isn't it? There is always time for the eternally human, but not for the outdated. Now you screw up your courage again and put forth that you would like to, once, venture into the domain of the time-sensitive if a tip or suggestion could be provided by the newspaper. Yes, but that's the thing about suggestions: newspapers like to *receive* them. They hope that you'll have a few the next time ... Then we go forth from the castle, and if we're in luck, in four weeks we'll find our brave little creation shrunk down to size in the paper. Our relations read it in detail and tell us their opinions. And a few experts even take notice.

Once one has been in print oneself, one takes a more vivid interest in other printed matter, and hangs around the book displays and carts. I ran into my bookseller at one of these barrows of late, a small black-haired doctor medicinae who presided over the peculiar house of books near the bridge.[2]

---

2   The editors of Hessel's collected works advise that the 'doctor medicinae' is Dr. Emil F. Tuchmann, his bookstore Bookhandlung Potsdamer Brücke near Hessel's place of employment at Rowohlt Verlag.

He was engaged in energetic conversation with the owner of the cart. I call him my bookseller because he cedes my modest literary requirements on credit, telling me everything that's in the books that I don't buy as part of the bargain. He also likes to watch as I leaf through the beautiful editions, which I certainly shan't acquire. If there aren't too many serious customers occupying him, sometimes he'll sit with me in the little back room and tell me about the fates of books and about the book trade. It's not exactly a time-sensitive subject. In earlier days, certain members of the profession were pleased to make bookshops a site of conversation, most recently the deceased Edmund Meyer, whose discussions and libations some bookmakers and book-lovers will remember. In today's hasty Berlin, such a thing hardly exists anymore. It's true that in some stores, the barrier that once separated buyer and seller has crumbled. One can walk around, sit, and stand as if in a friend's home library; and many of our bookshops follow the Munich example, calling themselves 'book parlours', 'book chambers', and the like. (There was even once a Book Bar, where two well-known celebrities played the part of the bartenders.) But the 'New Objectivity' doesn't allow contemplative lingering in these handsome rooms — much to the regret of those booksellers who themselves are book lovers. They would like to have customers in their shops who don't just want to be dealt with. They envy their Parisian colleagues, who enjoy a more convivial atmosphere, generally in more poorly furnished rooms, without their business suffering for it.

In America, whose conscious 'Objectivity' we otherwise

willingly imitate, there is said to be a sort of bookshop sociability. Now, when the Berliner has become more cosmopolitan and therefore more sedate, when he no longer prides himself on the fact that he 'doesn't get around to anything', then we will once again truly be welcomed as guests in the booksellers' chambers. The much-vaunted efficiency of the Berlin retail bookshop won't suffer the least for it, an efficiency outstripped neither by Paris nor any other cosmopolitan city. The Berlin bookseller is very well informed, and he will procure any acquirable book. The young are as good at it as the old; after all, they've grown up in the tradition, and study our nation's *Börsenblatt* enthusiastically each morning.[3] The big firms from the eighteenth century, Nicolai and Gsellius, have a well-established tradition, followed by Asher and Spaeth from the first half of the nineteenth.[4]

'Are there any true characters among the booksellers?' I once asked when the doctor was being a bit too thorough and factual for my likes. He thought a little, smiling impishly, but then didn't name any names. 'No,' he said, 'that only crops up among the antiquarian booksellers, if at all. Happy are those who have had the opportunity to spend an hour in conversation with Martin Breslauer,[5] the last of the learned, who still wore a real wing collar. We retail booksellers, we can't afford to be characters. We have to fight too hard for our existence, just like our good friends the publishers!'

'And is there much competition among yourselves?'

---

3   *Börsenblatt* is the industry magazine of the German book trade.
4   All prominent booksellers, some also publishers.
5   Breslauer was one of the most prominent 20th-century antiquarian booksellers worldwide.

'Not so much, but with the department stores, for example. That's a long story, though. I would have to give you a lecture on the definition of the word *junk* and its nuances. And on the conflict between the neutral modern organisation and the personal engagement demanded by objects of spiritual value.'

'Now, these wagons, the book carts, aren't they a stiff competition?'

'Oh no. That's a peculiar matter. First of all, it's often very strange people who push such carts, or have them pulled by a pony. Those people aren't shopkeepers. Some of them have led fantastical existences. Old actors, impoverished scholars, as well as fanatics of certain dispositions whose business interests often come second to their "cause". They're as varied as their clientele. Around carts like that, you'll see a chauffeur next to a bibliophile, curious shop girls next to an eager apprentice. In a certain sense, these carts work to our best interest. They bring books closer to the people than any display window can. And since the traffic police don't allow us — as is the case in happier countries — to lay our wares on the street, we must be thankful to the book carts for luring the customers into our shops, if in a roundabout fashion. They're a better advertisement for us than the National Book Day efforts could ever be.'

'Really, the writers themselves ought to stand on the street corners with their wares and cry: "Just ten copies left, written my very self, then they're all gone!"'

'People have already tried that sort of thing,' said the doctor. He didn't find it strange at all, and then he turned back to his gypsy colleague, to have a serious discussion about books.

The Southwest

'In the southwest, Wilmersdorf and Schöneberg have become completely conjoined with Berlin and Charlottenburg,' Baedeker informs us. Which is why we're not going to go in search of the precise borders, but rather we'll follow Potsdamer Straße past the Bülowstraße railway viaduct, arriving in the suburbs unawares.

First stop: the Sportpalast.

To see the people of Berlin in a fever, you must witness part of the 144 hours of the six-day race during which the bicyclists circle the angled wooden track. In the centre and box seating, you can observe high society, 'notables', prominent figures, and lovely shoulders in sable and fox. But if you want to sit among the true connoisseurs, among those whose participation is the most direct and Berlinesque, then you must sit among those in sweaters and anoraks in the gallery. No important score or lap goes unobserved there — their critique is the harshest, and it is there that you will hear the heartiest clapping. If 'nothing's happening' at the moment, they play cards. Then they cheer the riders on, hissing their favourites' first names. The riders actually aren't recognisable from up here without orienting one's self by their jersey colour and the number on their backs. You'll also undoubtedly have a sweet-natured neighbour who will indoctrinate you regarding the stages of the competition: the chases, turn-overs, penalty rounds, and sprints, as well as the meaning of the light signals: green = score, blue = prime, red = neutral lap. The Berliner is happy to inform you, however quaint it may seem to him that you don't know these crucial facts, which he himself learned as a little boy.

But when the controlled fury down there produces something remarkable, or when an important new lap begins, he'll turn away from you. Then he's all eyes and ears; he curses or cheers for this rider or that on whom he has placed a bet, either with his pals or in his heart. He forgets you, his friends, profession, and love; his pleasures and chagrins. Of the two great needs of the Roman people, *panis et circenses*, only the *circenses* still commands him today. Londoners and Parisians in sweaters and scarves are certainly also great sport enthusiasts, but they have a longer history of experience: in sport on the one hand, and in the pleasures of the big city on the other. But here you are sitting next to the newest big-city man. He is still unjaded, though he may pose coolly. He fevers along with these mass raptures. When the strike of the gong announces the top of a new hour, he awakens as if from a deep dream. For an instant, his glance strays from his rider's lane and grazes the device that shows the kilometres covered. You can see him in a paroxysm during sudden chases or on the final night, when his fire is stoked by the counting device at the finish line that displays the minutes left to ride.

But he's also entertaining in his milder moments. For example, when the ensemble plays something more worldly instead of one of his favourite pieces, which bores him. Then he gets worked up: 'Ey! Where's the "Sportpalast Waltz"? Ya corn-fed porkers! 'nother band please! An' shove it with yer "I Kiss Your … Madame".' When the ensemble does play the desired waltz, up here they whistle on their fingers and make special embellishments supporting the melody. The waiter's hoarse voice interjects: 'Who wants beer or lemonade?' A witty newspaper crier rhymes: 'The *Morg'npost*'ll cost ya a *groschen* at most.' Latecomers are greeted: 'Well lookit who's come round … well, y'old fairy, where ya bin hidin'? Boy, best y'eat more, ya bin pickled in formaldeehyde by the looks of it.'

A quiver jerks through the clouds of smoke and clusters of lamps: a rider has fallen. Was it a hard fall? No one knows yet. The others keep circling. The bleeding man is carried to the interior of the track on a stretcher. Maybe the masseur can help him now, so he won't require the doctor's station. The silk-clad ladies at the sekt table lean over the railing to stare at him. Then he's forgotten.

Such is the Sportpalast on one of its often and expertly recounted big nights. It has a beauty of its own during the six-day race, as well as during some of the calmer midday hours, when milky blue daylight falls onto the wooden track where the wheels hum quietly, illuminating the yellow and blue advertisements. That lends the wooden room a warmth and solidity that's otherwise seldom to be found in our Berlin.

Sports are international and they know no political parties. But their palace is also open to passions of the political variety. Big rallies for the National Socialists are announced. The halls fill. The police patrol in front of the doors, because counter-demonstrations are to be expected from 'the Reds' outside. And the distance between walking past and throwing punches is no farther than that between biting one's thumb and drawing one's weapon for the Montagues and Capulets. All at once, it's claimed that the communists are trying to storm the palace. The police receive reinforcements. Rubber batons are being swung. It's hard to determine who instigated it. If they weren't wearing their insignia, the Order of Reaction or Revolution, they could hardly be distinguished, these brash Berlin lads from both camps. From time to time, members of the Stahlhelm are known to lurk outside while the Reds convene within. Then the auditorium is hung with bright-red banners with slogans. Again and again, the fire marshals must make sure the stairway isn't blocked. Chairs are carried over and jammed together. From the balcony boxes up top to the doorway down below, everything is full. The crowd steps docilely to the side when the Rotfront makes its entrance. The music is martial, which excites the party members, as it once did when they were also comrades in arms. Very young boys advance, striking cymbals. Pipers follow them in lockstep. The men greet the flags with clenched fists, the boys with open hands.

The Sportpalast peacefully tolerates all of this with a sort of gargantuan good-naturedness. Its walls impartially echo 'Swastika on the helmet' and 'This is the final struggle', just as they do the cries of the sports fans.[1] All of it is the exuberance

---

1   Lyrics from 'Hakenkreuz am Stahlhelm' (a popular song among Nazi-sympathisers in the Weimar Republic) and 'The Internationale', respectively.

of the same unceasing lust for life.

Next stop: Heinrich von Kleist Park.

Gontard's colonnades provide a special flourish there, but they used to stand near where the Alexanderplatz train station is today. They're not yet entirely at home here in the fabric of the city, as the colonnades by the same master at the end of Leipziger Straße are. Their curves open onto a plaza-like space, a peaceful piece of past in the loudest of business districts. (It's as if the open doors and gates behind the columns were portals to the rooms of time gone by.) In this park, these displaced colonnades really should be ruins, or at least more weathered. At the very least, someone should make sure there are birds' nests in them ... In any case, we delight at the carved wreaths around the scrollwork capitals and the reliefs below, which remind me of bookplate scenes. One of the statues is a plump nymph girl who, for all of the rococo-antique in her expression, still has something of the Berlin 'streetwalker' about her — an idea far older than that turn of phrase. A female archer aims at the centre of the park as gracefully as possible, across the lily pond and toward the remaining flora from the botanic garden that was relocated out beyond Steglitz. The children aren't allowed near the blossoms cropping up between the small stones — they have to stay in the sandboxes, or steer their scooters down the broad path. The happiest children may be those who are sliding down the sand heap next to the plank fence along the excavated water pipes. Of the adults present, we take the greatest interest in the group of card players on the bench under the foliage. I think they're unemployed, like those we saw in Friedrichshain.

For a few hours, they forget their misery. They look anxiously at the cards in the hands of the man who is shuffling, just as Rembrandt's doctors stare at the corpse under the instructor's knife in *The Anatomy Lesson*. A paralytic has rolled his cart up to the game on the bench and is passionately playing the backseat driver.

Now we're entering Schöneberg proper. Hauptstraße has everything, even buildings with onion-like domes and staircases for gentlemen only. And shops with double burners, and lunch-tins with adjustable compartments, and other such practical necessities. We have no desire to linger. Being around here makes a person extraordinarily sad. Let's walk across Kaiser Wilhelm Platz — what else would it be called? — into the officially sad district of Schöneberg, the 'Island', as its residents call the area where the streets sidle up to the circle-line railway. In the mornings and evenings, you can observe hurried, impoverished people walking through the 'Polish Corridor' between the Schöneberg and Großgörschenstraße train stations,[2] which aren't connected to each other. Behind the sorry facades, one divines sunless courtyards, so-called 'lawns' where the children aren't allowed to dig, rubbish bins, the inadvertent duet of a radio in a window and a barrel organ down below, screeching neighbours, and the thin voice of a singing beggar. The red-draped stand there on the corner of the side street houses a propaganda office of the KPD, who can count on a warm reception here. The tram takes a hilly path

---

2   Julius-Leber-Brücke Station is in a nearby location to then-Schöneberg Station, while Großgörschenstraße is the Yorkstraße Station on the S1 line today.

from Tempelhof across the train tracks, between the freight station and waste disposal sheds. It carries us quickly to the other end of Schöneberg, to the deep trough of the Schöneberg City Park.[3] If necessary, one could pinpoint the location of the lovers' song 'Schöneberg in the Month of May' here, which is hardly imaginable anywhere else in this district, with a promising name like that.

North of the City Park is the much admired 'Bavarian Quarter'. How much of it should be ascribed to Berlin, Schöneberg, or Wilmersdorf, I don't know. It's not so right-angled and straight-lined as western Berlin. And instead of being thankful, we curse the fact that we're constantly getting lost among all these Heilbronns and Regensburgs and Landshuts and Aschaffenburgs.[4] No one can do right by us. We also tolerate the many fountains and copses, without really paying them any attention. On some corners, we stumble over attempts to imitate an old German city. The failure is heartwarming. You can't be too hard on the Bavarian Quarter. When it was built, our true deliverer and great equaliser, the conveyor belt of industrialisation, didn't yet exist.

The long Kaiserallee leads through Wilmersdorf and Friedenau, surrounded by residential areas that grew out of old villages and villa colonies. It's said that Friedenau is a refuge for former royal officials and now-pensionless pensioners of the old school, as is certainly the case for parts of Steglitz and Lichterfelde. Creatures who sport a chronically indignant

---

3   Known as Rudolph Wilde Park today.
4   Street names in the Bavarian Quarter.

expression under beards that seem left over from an earlier era; who were born to be privy councillors and legal clerks; they are accompanied by spouses who often have real feathers on their hats, as the ladies of the world wore them in yesteryear. These peculiar matrons dwell in welcoming if somewhat outmoded houses with gardens. One imagines that, in their cosy homes, they must become more loving than they seem. At least we'd like to hope for the sake of their children ...

Steglitz begins where Schloßstraße[5] meets Kaiserallee. This beginning is highly modern: light flows through glowing tubes along the flanks of the towering cinema palace; inside, stark lines and bold curves circumscribe the stage and auditorium. But our good Steglitz is one of the older Berlin villages, and many of the buildings on the side streets that lead to the City Park have been left as they were around the turn of the century. Back then, one visited school and university friends here, outliers who needed the tranquillity of this far-flung suburb to better comprehend the cosmopolitan city. The oldest building here is the Schloßpark restaurant with its theatre, erected just after 1800 by David Gilly as a country estate.

We reach the next station on the Wannsee Railway,[6] the Botanical Garden. It's a wondrous creation of science and aesthetics where you can ramble through the flora of the high mountains in tiny alps and cordilleras. You can traipse through all of the Carpathians in half a minute. The Mediterranean isn't far from the Himalayas. But behind the palm house, our native

5   Called Bundesallee today.
6   Now part of the S1 line.

hill, the Dahlem Fichtenberg, rises. The streets and squares around the garden have pretty names. There's a Begonienplatz, an Asternplatz, and a Malvenstraße.

The research institutions of near-lying Dahlem are well situated at the edge of the garden, along with the Botanical Museum and the Museum of Plant Physiology. Pure science resides in the sunlit summer homes of biology, entomology, ethnology, and chemistry. The agricultural institute sits comfortably in a sort of manor house. Even the Prussian Privy State Archives, located here, have fresh country colours and a festive red roof. In Dahlem, the subway stations themselves have a summery charm. This suburb is one of the areas where the Berliner of tomorrow lives, a breed in whom the exhaustion of their fathers, who 'didn't get around to anything' because they had too much to do, seems to be transformed into a carefree flexibility. Now, we don't want to claim anything with certainty, but we can hope.

Maybe we'll be lucky and chance to meet one of the young lady Berliners of Dahlem. She has parked her car here in front of the lovely cafe at the station, and comes with us on foot into the forest up to Lake Krumme Lanke and then along the water to Onkel Toms Hütte,[7] or to the old Grunewald hunting lodge, which Kaspar Theiss built long ago for Prince Joachim. We spend a while in front of the curious stone relief depicting three people standing around a table: in the middle, the potbellied prince as innkeeper or vintner with his sleeves rolled up; next to him, a master builder in courtly attire who is being served a

---

7   A housing estate by architect Bruno Taut.

tankard by his lord; and a third figure who holds a stein already filled with more drink. We puzzle over the funny verses in old German beneath it. But soon we have enough of tip-toeing through the old times, and the courteous Dahlem lady drives us at a frantic pace to the new estate on Riemeisterstraße, to the streets of old Lichterfeld villas, and toward Zehlendorf. There, in the midst of all of everything new and newer, the octagonal village church with its pointed roof from the days of Friedrich the Great exerts a moment's fascination. Then we continue through Schlachtensee and Nikolassee to Wannsee. We take our tea in a somewhat remote house on the lake. A little ensemble entices us to dance a bit. Our guide informs us about the part of Berlin's high society that takes part in the new summer fashions. But she's also in the know about sailboats. She's familiar with the owner of a pretty yacht, knows to whom the zealous motorboat belongs. Maybe we still have time to drive to Stölpchensee and look down at the paddleboats from the terrace, at the young, delicately powerful knees of the girls who lie sunken deep in the boat while their companions steer. While driving past the Schildhorn peninsula, we see the people who've taken the bus here to swim in the open air, toss balls around, and frolic with their dogs. It's stirring, the sight of the dune-soft sand at the edge of the forested slope, where unkempt paths wander between rabbit holes.

Perhaps our guide is a member of the golf club and will take us with her, if we've earned it, to those most beautiful athletic grounds. To describe it, I'll cite the poet of this lively, modern Berlin, Wilhelm Speyer in his book *Charlott, a Little Crazy*:

Among the new sports facilities that had entered Berlin's life recently, none had turned out finer than the golf course between Wannsee and Potsdam. Swathes of lawn and forests of fir are dotted with sidelong bungalows sloping in gentle north-German fashion to a small lake or to new forests and new lawns. Viewed from the clubhouse terrace, the far-flung players and their colourfully clothed caddies seem densely concentrated through the dry, clear Brandenburg air before the observer's field of vision, as if they, with their raised or lowered equipment, were figures depicted in the luxuriant reduction of a Japanese woodcarving. Accompanied only by a boy bag-bearer, secluded from the other players, there is something in the player's posture that suggests the pious, self-reliant zeal of one of the Thebaid hermits.

Our guide gives names to several such figures while we sit on the pretty terrace, and so we get to know Berlin's elite. It's a difficult-to-delineate entity formed by the accrual of so many different and peculiar ambitions that the resulting society is simultaneously the freest and the most conventional. Tremendous composure is required to let one's hair down as the greatest Berliners do. Via our Athena (Athena being the goddess of the young female Berliners, more so than Diana or Venus, I believe), yes, via our Athena we'll also get to know the man who takes us with him to polo in the garden city of Frohnau, to harness racing in Mariendorf, to the racecourse in Grunewald, and so on.

After all of that, to round off her benevolence, she also drives us home, along the Automobile Traffic and Training

Road, at that. There, we learn that we're not yet as well versed as any ten-year-old boy, who can distinguish various well-known automobiles as they pass. In some cases — such as this big Hispano, that elegant Buick, this svelte all-red one, or that little all-white car — Athena even names the owner or the lady at the wheel, while the small trees behind the fence and the advertisements at the edge of the road sink aslant behind our swiftness. We glide more slowly through the northern gate, then once again at eighty or more kilometres per hour beyond the radio tower and down the broad street leading up to Tiergarten.

Afterword

These were a few shy attempts to go walking in Berlin, round about and through the middle. Now, dear fellow citizens, please don't reproach me for all of the important and noteworthy things that I've overlooked; rather, go out yourselves, aimlessly, just as I have done, on hazard's little voyages of discovery. You don't have time? That's false ambition speaking.

Give a little of your love of landscape to the city! I've said nothing here about landscape, and I've only gone beyond the city limits briefly with a few words. It has already been described and painted so often, this strange land in which our city dwells, this Brandenburg landscape that has retained something prehistoric about it right up to the present day. As soon as the Sunday visitors have left them, pine forests, swamp, and sand are precisely as they were before the first settlers, particularly to the east. In the west, we have a bit of landscape that a human hand has also sculpted. That's the area that Georg Hermann called an enclave of the south in his *Walk in Potsdam*.[1] As to how the cityscape and parkscape insinuated itself into this virgin soil of the eighteenth century, you'll just have to read in the little book. And then let him show you the square by the City Palace, the 'dissociated dream of architecture', Knobelsdorff's

---

1 *Spaziergang in Potsdam*. Rembrandt-Verlag, Berlin: 1926.

colonnades in the palace garden, and the giant columns with delicately perforated balustrades, as well as the palaces, hedges, and flower beds of Sanssouci. He illuminates the personal aspects of this royal creation, understands the way in which Friedrich 'determined the overall form of the city, as if he had always had its entirety before his mind's eye'. Arm-in-arm with this guide, you'll be well-equipped to wander the streets of the city with their happy vistas and obstructions, to live among all of the vases, garlands, flutes, and lyres, the coats of arms and sphinxes of the architectural sculptures, which 'even [have] cupids patching nets on the roof peaks in the district where the fishers live'. Hermann distinguishes between different types of buildings: cherub buildings, vase buildings, urn, mask, medallion, garland, and Wedgwood buildings, and their compound forms, describing one old street that 'is a twittering aviary of all these types'. Wherever he leads us, he serenely practises what he himself calls the 'peripatetic study of style'.

Fontane leads us into the near and more distant Havelland. From him, we read about the history of the Pfaueninsel and how it looked more recently, for example. The flowered wallpaper, bed canopies, and furniture from the world of Queen Luise lead to similar patterns in the village of Paretz. The hanging and dripping trees on the wall tapestries, and the commodes and divans all still contain so much of the atmosphere of this woman's world.

It's not difficult to love these perfect Potsdam beauties, but we must learn to love the beauty of Berlin. To close, now, I really should also confess a few of my 'formational experiences'. And

I should disclose which books have told me the things that can't be seen with the eye, along with the ones that have taught me to see better some of the things I *have* seen. So a small closing bibliography would give my book a little of the dignity that it lacks. Oh, but even in the libraries and collections, I was led more by the adventure of chance than by proper scholarship, and I wouldn't want to lure anyone else onto such a tangled path through the world of books.

One of the great experts on history, culture, and art in Berlin (you'll find his name in the Baedeker literature section) once wanted to compose a description of the city using only old descriptions, with all of the monuments described by close contemporaries from the time of their creation: Rector Küster of the Friedrichswerdersche Secondary School would have had his say about the tomb of Minister of State Johann Andreas Kraut in St. Nicolas's Church; the musical journeys in the diary of Doctor Charles Burney would have been cited for their depiction of the opera house. As for describing the works of Schinkel, he would have selected one of those people who referred to Schinkel as Royal Privy Senior Building Officer, and so on. It would have resulted in a delightful bibliographical walk through Berlin that made new pasts for the city accessible to us and taught us to enjoy those aspects that have already disappeared.

To date, perhaps Berlin hasn't really been loved enough, as a great friend of the city, Mayor Reiche, once complained. You can still sense that many parts of Berlin haven't been viewed enough to truly be visible. We Berliners must dwell in our city to a much greater degree. It's not at all easy, neither the viewing nor the dwelling in a city that is incessantly on the go, always in the middle of becoming something different and never at rest in yesterday's form. In his brilliant but hopefully too-pessimistic book *Berlin: Destiny of a City*, Karl Scheffler complains that today Berlin is still, as centuries ago, a truly colonial city, shoved out on the empty steppe. With no tradition around it, and therefore so much impatience and unrest. How can we expect its residents to linger affectionately in the present and take on the benign role of staffage in the image of the city?

Let us believe ourselves capable of it, let us learn a bit of idleness and indulgence, and look at the thing that is Berlin, in its combination and chaos of luxury and meanness, solidity and spuriousness, peculiarity and respectability, until we become fond of it and find it beautiful, until it is beautiful.